SYBIL SHACK Saturday's Stepchildren: Canadian Women in Business

---

Monday's child is fair of face,
Tuesday's child is full of grace,
Wednesday's child is full of woe,
Thursday's child has far to go,
Friday's child is loving and giving,
Saturday's child works hard for a living . . .

Anon.

Guidance Centre   Faculty of Education   University of Toronto

*I should like to dedicate
this book to my mother
who was in her time a
very good business-
woman.*

ISBN: 0-7713-0025-5

Contents

Preface

This book is not intended to be a profound sociological study, a detailed examination of causes and effects, or an in-depth analysis of motivations and attitudes. It is rather a personal report of the feelings, thoughts, and experiences of businesswomen, and sometimes of their employers, as they were shared with me in writing and conversation by nearly one hundred and fifty women and men in a period of a little over a year.

I am grateful to all these people who have been so generous with their time, their thoughtful exposition of their ideas, and their continuing interest in this project. The book is theirs.

I am also grateful to women at Canada Manpower in Winnipeg and Toronto; to women in the Women's Bureau of the federal Department of Labour; to women in the provincial departments of labour and in the Ontario Ministry of Labour; to administrators and teachers at the community colleges who went to great lengths to provide me with information and to arrange interviews for me with business education students; to administrators and teachers in the high schools I visited and to the students in these institutions. I wish I could name them all to show my appreciation of their help and co-operation.

A special thanks is due to June Menzies, until recently western regional vice-chairman of the Advisory Council on the Status of Women, and to her assistant, Eleanor Milne. It was through their good offices that I was able to reach many of the women who answered my questionnaire and whom I interviewed across the country.

I must also acknowledge the support of the Canada Council. A Council grant under the Explorations program enabled me to extend my personal contacts and visits beyond my home province of Manitoba.

I have made considerable use of a questionnaire designed to give me a mental picture of the respondent – her background, interests, and business career – and a synopsis of her opinions of and experiences in the business world. The women who answered often wrote me letters that expressed fervently their feelings about failures and triumphs, their enthusiasms and complaints. From time to time I have taken the liberty of condensing and consolidating ideas and opinions that were common to large numbers of my correspondents and attributing them to a composite person. Occasionally at the request of the persons concerned I have disguised names and changed enough of the detail of their information to protect their anonymity. Where both first and family names have been used, however, in almost all cases I am quoting real people who indicated their willingness to be quoted.

If I have misunderstood, misinterpreted, or misquoted any of the many people whose expertise I have drawn upon, I ask them to accept my apologies.

SYBIL SHACK

The towers of the city cut interesting geo- metric patterns in the deep blue of the morn- ing sky. The orange buses converge from all directions, squeal to a stop, and pour their contents onto pavements already warming with the promise of the day. High boots, bulky platform soles, thong-held sandals patter as red lights turn to green on busy corners. The breeze stirs long loose hair, tugs at well-sprayed coiffures, rumples little curls.

1

Women at Work: An Overview

Pant suits, slacks, swirling skirts, long, short, and shorter; handbags, shoulder bags, tote bags, shopping bags, lunch bags, shoe bags; scarves and bright blouses; coats and sweaters in every shade and tint flow and mingle and separate to be swallowed in the huge blocks of concrete.

Inside, the elevators slide silently, carrying their bright cargoes, until by nine o'clock the buses and the streetcars and the subways are emptied, cars have been stowed away, and the buildings are filled. A clanging bell announces to waiting customers that shops are open. Covers have come off typewriters; vaults have been opened; merchandise is ready for sale. In every part of the city and all over the country women are beginning their day in business: in stores and offices, in banks and insurance companies, in small dark cubbyholes with battered desks and single telephones, and in huge complexes with hundreds of desks and computerized systems.

I walk into one of these offices. In my line of vision I count eleven women at work. Most of them have typewriters in front of them, and, as I watch, their fingers fly over the keyboards. I cannot hear them; the ceiling, I note, has been acoustically treated, lowered in what had once been a dark high noisy space. Under foot, carpet absorbs the sound of my steps and the noise of the machines.

A man is saying something to one of the women. Although they are only three or four feet from me, they might be deaf mutes for all the sound that reaches me.

The young woman who comes to the counter to greet me is tall, slender, with long, loose, light brown hair that floats and shines in the artificial light. Her face is pleasant and pretty with the freshness of youth and good nature. She listens patiently as I explain my problem – not as succinctly as I might – excuses herself for a moment while she confers with someone, and comes back to me with a satisfactory answer. I ask her whether I may talk with her personally during her coffee break, and we meet an hour later in the company cafeteria. In the fifteen minutes we have together at a corner table I learn a good deal about Julie.

Is this her first job, I ask. She looks so young!

No, as a matter of fact it is her third.

She is twenty-three, she tells me. She lived with her family in a small house in a Toronto suburb until she went to work, when she moved into an equally small apartment within easy travelling distance of the down-town area. "Bus, subway, you know." She shares the apartment with two other girls. Currently one is a nurse who is on a night shift. "That helps," Julie says. "That way we're not all needing the bathroom in the morning at the same time." Sharing helps with the rent. The rent is way out of line, far more than one girl alone could manage.

Their social life? Well, they don't really see that much of one another. They have their own interests. She has a boy friend. The other two don't at the moment. But it's nice to have someone there in case you're sick or something. The arrangement has worked out quite well, though Julie is the only one of the original three still in the apartment. She thinks the present lot will stay together until one of them gets married.

She had taken a business course at high school and brushed up her typing and shorthand ("I don't know why I bothered with the short-hand; I've never used it") at a private business college during the summer months following her last year at school – Grade 11. She had then stepped into a job with no trouble at all. "My father knew someone who had a small jobbing company. The man needed a girl who was willing to work on Saturday mornings and wasn't asking too much money. I went to see him and was hired on the spot. I kind of liked the job. Because I was the only girl I did so many different things; there was never a dull moment. I got to know all kinds of people on the telephone, and I used to try to guess what they looked like. Sometimes I got to see them and sometimes I didn't. There was one fellow who had a beautiful rich voice, deep and romantic. I almost died when I saw him for the first time. He was a little runt of a chap with a skinny moustache. I'll bet he didn't weigh more than 110 pounds! He told me he had eight children, and he couldn't have been more than thirty years old!"

What made her decide to take a business course?

"Well, my mother worked at Eaton's and never got very far because she wasn't trained to do anything different. I decided that I had to be able to do something more than just sell notions or lingerie or what have you. My older sister was working in an office, so I just naturally took business ed."

Had she ever wanted to do anything else?

"Well, not really. You know, I always thought it would be fun to be a stewardess or something glamorous like that. But I didn't think I could make it. I expect I'll get married and work for a while. My boy friend has a job with the transit company. He doesn't want me to work after we are married, but I think I will, at least until we get our furniture and things." The small diamond on her left hand is very much in evidence.

She'd left the jobbing company because after a while she was finding it lonely in the office, and besides, her friends were all getting more money than she was. She answered an advertisement in the paper and was hired.

"That job I hated," she said, making a face at the very thought of it. "I was one girl in at least two hundred. We sat at desks in long rows with fluorescent lights shining on us all day long. Fifteen minutes for coffee break. An hour for lunch. I didn't even get to know the girls sitting on either side of me. We worked like machines. I don't think anyone knew my name except the payroll clerk, and he just knew my name, not my face. I got out of there as fast as I could."

Again she had answered an advertisement in the paper, and this time she found something she really likes. "It's quiet in here; the boss of our department is a nice guy. He never yells at you. I do two or three different things and handle some pretty confidential information as well as meeting the public. You see, I look after the counter, answer questions, and deal with telephone calls to the department. When the calls are simple inquiries I answer them myself. When I don't know the answers it's my business to give the calls to people who do know. My boss passed along a compliment the other day. A lady had told him how pleasant I was on the telephone, and how efficiently I had answered her questions. That made me feel pretty good."

Did the company offer any benefits? "I don't really know," she answered. "I get my three weeks' holiday, now that I've been here three years." Pension? "Oh, gosh," she laughed. "I'm not worried about that! Something is taken off my cheque, but I don't really know how much or what happens to it. Gee, my *mother* has twenty years to go before she gets a pension. Why should I be worrying about a pension?"

Is she interested in promotion, in doing other kinds of work? She looks at me blankly. What do I mean? Getting to be a "boss"? Heavens, no! She's getting married, and she'll have children, she hopes. She a manager? She laughs again.

In Julie's immediate work area I had noticed six young women and two young men. What did the young men do? "Not as much as I do, that I can tell you," Julie says. "They sure spend a lot of time looking busy. When they have to type something – not very often – they pick out the words with four fingers, and they yell for us when they want a folder. We tell them what's in it, and then they talk about it to the customer." Julie is obviously not very impressed with the young men. "They come and go," she says. "They're never here more than a few months. Then they're transferred, and we don't see them again. Every once in a while one of them turns up looking very high class in a vest – a proper suit – and we know he has made it somewhere or other. What'll you bet they get paid a lot more than we do, at that?"

That was a bet I knew it wasn't safe to take.

Julie does not think so now, but the chances are good that she will work a lot longer than the few months she is counting on after she is married. Right now she is one of the 1,119,000 women working in clerical jobs in this country. Even in 1974, two-thirds of the women working in all of Canada were twenty-five years old and over, and 57.1 per cent of all women working were married. Another healthy segment (9.1 per cent) consisted of women who were divorced, separated, or widowed.[1] It may well be that, in spite of what her boy friend now thinks about her working, she will be back in the labour force as soon as she believes she can leave her children. If she works even briefly after their marriage, she and her husband may find it difficult to manage on one income, especially if they have two or three children to raise. Many a young husband has changed his mind about his wife working when he discovers that it is not, in fact, as cheap for two to live as it is for one, and that the addition of two or three children's mouths to feed raises the cost of living a great deal more. Besides, the wants and needs that have been established earlier are hard to change, and Julie's addition to the family budget may be attractive indeed, especially if her husband's status with the transit company does not change radically and his income rises only in proportion to the cost of living. So what to Julie now seems a temporary excursion into the world of business may indeed become a lifetime career, broken perhaps for a few years while she is at home looking after her children, but likely to spread over twenty-five or thirty years or more.

Zetta Rykiss was in a position much like Julie's when she started out on her career. We have been friends for a long time, since before her first marriage during the Second World War. She is in her middle fifties, the mother of two children, a daughter and a son, both successful

4

in their chosen careers. For more than twenty years she has worked for a large corporation, beginning as a stenographer. She is now private secretary to one of the senior men in the company.

"Was business my first career choice? Definitely not! I wanted to be a dancer (how I loved to dance!). I wanted to be a long-distance swimmer (by the time I was twelve I was a very strong swimmer). I wanted to be a kindergarten teacher (I loved being with youngsters). I wanted to learn to play the piano (I could pick out a song by ear by the time I was seven). So how did it happen that I ended up in the business world for twenty-six years? After all, it wasn't so unreasonable of me to want these things. I knew I could be good at doing them."

Why hadn't she at least tried them?

"To begin with," she said, "I grew up poor, though we never in our family thought of ourselves in that way. Then, I was born in 1920, the third of five children, the eldest being a boy.

"Our parents knew that they wouldn't be able to send all of us to university. They felt that it was most important for the boy to have the best education possible in order to equip him to make the best possible living in our social structure and become a proper future provider for a future wife and family. Girls were expected to get as much education as possible – my parents were actually education worshippers, like most Jewish parents – but since eventually girls married, and women were not expected to work after marriage, it would be a 'waste of money' to send them to university, especially when money was scarce, and it certainly was scarce in those times and in my family.

"So my brother went to university and graduated as an architect, the girls to Grade 11 or 12 and then to work.

" 'Work' for a girl usually meant being a 'saleslady.' A saleslady was what you ended up being if you had no trade or education or were unable to get a position in whatever field you were trained in, and even then you were lucky to be a saleslady. After all, you were working. Jobs were hard to get, whether you were qualified or not, and doubly so for girls, since job choices for girls were very limited. By the time I was in Grade 9 I had decided to try to be a stenographer, take a commercial course in Grades 10 and 11, maybe go to a business college, and get a job in an office. This, I felt, was a far better way to make a living than being a saleslady.

"Like most women in the late 1930s and the 1940s, when I was married and started my family I stopped working and became a housewife. I had no intention of going back into business, because 'a woman's place was at home with husband and children.' The only time a woman went to work outside her home was when there were financial difficulties.

"Well, in 1954 things turned out so that I had absolutely no choice. I had to go back to work. My husband was ill, and we both knew that his time was limited. So naturally I looked for the kind of job in which I had the most experience, in an office. Now if I had had the same opportunities as my brother had had, and a better education than I did have, how easy it would have been to take care of our financial needs at home! However, being a stenographer was the only profession I knew, and so back into the business world, and this time I stayed."

Zetta's husband died, and some years later she married again. She is a young and energetic grandmother, but she is still at work. I asked her, as I asked many others, how satisfying her work was, what pleasure she derived from it.

"When I first began working again in 1954 I had no time to think of my work as satisfying me," she said. "I was only interested in doing my job to the best of my ability and satisfying my employers. To tell the truth, my getting satisfaction out of the work I was doing never entered my head, but satisfying my employers meant good, permanent employment, and in that I was very interested. I knew that I needed the employment, not that the employer needed me."

"What about now?" I asked. "How do you feel now?"

"I suppose," she answered me, "as the years have gone by I've found satisfaction in doing my job well, being capable of doing it well, and in being promoted because of doing it well. I also realize that I have learned a lot and have been able to improve myself by being in the business world, something I would not have been able to do, I think, while staying at home."

For example?

"For example, I have learned to spell, broadened my vocabulary, learned to think quickly and clearly, learned to make decisions. In fact, you could say that I have been getting an education while working."

Scores of other women have given me similar answers. They went to work because they had to, because they needed the money, to maintain themselves and their families. For a long time it did not occur to them that anyone but their employers had the right to profit from their labours. As one woman wrote to me, in response to some questions I asked her, "Thank you for sending me your questionnaire. It made me sit down and think, probably for the first time in my life, about what I was doing. Yes, I get a great deal of satisfaction out of my work, though

6

my family and my friends might not think so when they hear me crabbing about how tired I am, and how much I look forward to my vacation. I keep books. The work is very detailed, and I have to be meticulous about it. But it gives me tremendous satisfaction to have everything come out even. I feel proud when the income tax people congratulate me on my books. It would be nice, I admit, if my employer occasionally told me how good I am. He doesn't, and the raises have been few and far between, and I have to ask for them. It doesn't occur to him that I too need money to live on, and that I would like to live just as nicely as my married sisters whose husbands have done very well. Oh, well, I guess I am really one of the lucky ones. I can afford to drive a car, and I have an apartment of my own. Some of my friends who are just as smart as I am are stuck in dead-end jobs they don't enjoy at all."

One of the "salesladies" I spoke with works in the bargain basement of a large department store. She had left school at sixteen to help out at home; her mother was a widow. She is thirtyish, attractive, and like my previous correspondent unmarried. She said to me, "I love what I am doing even if I am dead tired when I get home at night. The concrete floor feels pretty hard after eight hours of standing on it! But I am with people all day long. The girls I work with are grand. We give one another a hand whenever we can. The customers are always interesting. We get such variety in our store. In the last few years there have been a lot of immigrant women. Most of them work in the factories a block or two from the store and pop in for a little shopping during the lunch hour. I love to listen to them, and I have been amazed at how quickly some of them have learned to speak English and think like Canadians. You get to know the regulars, of course, the people who come in two or three times a week. I'll put aside a bargain sometimes for a woman, and she's always so grateful."

She looked surprised when I asked her whether she expected a promotion to section head, or department manager, or whatever. "Oh, no," she said. "That's not for me. We did have a woman manager for a while, and she was pretty good, too. She's upstairs now somewhere. But she's the only one we ever had. The managers are all men."

A buyer, perhaps?

Well, she didn't know anything about that, or who did the buying for her department. The goods were there. She had worked in several other departments of the store, and liked them too. She preferred being in a busy department; she didn't want to stand around doing nothing or gossiping with the girls.

I taught Olga once, some years ago. She now works part time at a check-out counter in a large supermarket. "It's just what I need," she told me. "It gets me out of the house. I can book off if the kids are sick or my husband has his holidays. The hours are right for me because they fit in with Michael's shift; he looks after the kids, gives them their lunch, and sends them off to school on the days when I am at work. Sure it's hard work, and goodness knows the pay isn't much, but it helps out a little, and I'm glad to have it. You know me. I wasn't much for studying, but I was a good little kid at school. My parents brought me up to do what I was told. In my job I don't have to do much thinking or figuring; the cash register does it for me. Maybe when the children are older I'll take on full-time work."

Had she ever thought of going back to school to equip herself for a different kind of job that might pay more? She had not been a brilliant student at school, but she had not been dull either. Other places – for example, the city or the provincial government – pay better than the supermarket, and when she is ready for full-time work she might do what another pupil of mine, a friend of hers, had done: she might get a job as a filing clerk or a clerk-typist. She would have some security, better pay, a pension, and the work would not be as heavy, physically.

"Yes," she said, "I've thought about it, and maybe I'll do it – when the kids are a little older and can be left all day. Michael keeps on telling me I am a sucker, that I shouldn't be working at the minimum wage, that I am too good for what I am doing. It's nice he thinks I'm that good, but I'm scared. I don't think I'm good. Besides, I'd feel silly sitting there in the school with young kids." Then she added defiantly, "Anyway, I like what I am doing, and right now I don't want to work full time."

Olga is one of the 36 per cent of women in the labour force who work less than thirty-five hours a week, that is, the part-time workers. By contrast, only 18 per cent of the total male labour force worked part time in 1974.[2]

I do not know that Olga is too good for the job she is doing, as her husband says. It is a perfectly respectable and necessary job and one that she obviously enjoys "because I see so many people. I have regular customers who'll stand in line just to go through my check-out." On the other hand, she is a conscientious, pleasant, helpful, efficient woman. If she is to stay at the check-out counter for the rest of her working life, she is entitled to more than she has now: insecurity of tenure, poor pay, no provision for the future.

Is her store unionized? Not yet. Her Michael tells her that she should be pushing for a union. He's a union man, of course, and knows the benefits that can accrue. "That's right. But, gee, Miss Shack, I don't think I could ever go on strike or fight. Do you remember when the other stores were striking and there was picketing and everything? Gee, that's not for me. Yeah, I'm a sissy and a ninny. That's what Michael tells me."

Gladys Neale is one of the few women I know whose career is in the male Horatio Alger tradition; she started out at the bottom and now holds a top management position. Smartly dressed, handsome, energetic, and well-organized, she is acknowledged to be an outstanding and knowledgeable person in educational publishing in Canada. She is interested and involved in professional and community affairs in spite of the long hours she spends at her work. She travels extensively on this continent and abroad both for pleasure and on business. In fact, she is a female counterpart of the successful male executive in a highly com- petitive field. Yet she is by no means "masculine," whatever image that adjective conjures up when it is used to describe a woman.

She is a director and vice-president of Macmillan of Canada, a lead- ing publishing house, and is head of its educational division. When Macmillan was purchased a few years ago by Maclean-Hunter, Gladys Neale became a vice-president of that company as well and is in charge of its instructional materials division.

What started her off on her business career?

"School teaching," she said. "It was difficult to get a permanent job teaching, and substitute teaching was rough then as it is now. While I was at school I worked as a page in a public library and decided that I wanted to work with books, and so I went after a job in publishing."

She went after it, and she got it. It was a routine clerical job. From that beginning she worked her way through five different categories. When her immediate superior enlisted during the Second World War, she took over his work for the duration. By that time she had proved her worth, her ability to get things done. She was so good that she was put in charge of the textbook section of the publishing house. As with most Canadian publishers, this section had been the moneymaking part of the business. The revenue it brings in enables publishers to take risks with other possibly more prestigious and less profitable publishing ventures.

"Extremely satisfying work," is Miss Neale's assessment of what she does. "It is personally and professionally satisfying to make a contribution to Canadian culture and to the education of Canadian children and young people; to develop an idea for a book and to see it published; and – yes, to have books which are successful in the marketplace."

She could also have added that it is personally and professionally rewarding to find and encourage potential Canadian writers of Canadian textbooks for Canadian children.

Had she encountered any special difficulties in attaining the position she now holds?

Her answer: "I think it's fair to say that it has been a battle sometimes to have my abilities recognized. Men, whether consciously or not, have been and still are prejudiced against women in business and would prefer to promote men rather than women. On the other hand, in my career I have done a lot of travelling and have been accorded privileges and courtesies by business contacts which probably would not have been given to men. Then I have had more co-operation, support, and help from my family than most people have."

Gladys Neale is that rare person, a woman who has reached the upper ranks of private business in Canada. In 1974 only 2.7 per cent of working women were in managerial positions of any kind in this country, and most of these held jobs in the lower levels of management.[3] If trends here and in the United States are to be believed, the percentage is declining rather than increasing in the upper levels, though slightly more women are making it in the lower and middle management ranges. For example, figures for 1972 showed 4 per cent of women workers in management and administration.[4] Very few women are, like Gladys Neale, working vice-presidents of their companies. Those who are are likely to be working in family businesses. Female presidents are even rarer. They are likely to be the major shareholders in the companies over which they preside; that is, they are really self-employed.

What about women who are self-employed? I could get no information regarding their numbers, but I have met many of them over the years, most of them happy, alert, interested human beings. Take Faye Settler as an example. Slender, quick-moving, quick-thinking, a very young grandmother, she has a wide range of interests.

Faye operates a successful retail art gallery and antique shop in downtown Winnipeg. I have known her family for a long time and remember vividly visiting in her parents' home when Faye was a little girl. It was a fascinating place. I recall my pleasure at exploring its treasures. The walls of the entrance hall were almost covered with pictures, prints, postcards, etchings of Queen Victoria. Faye's mother at that time was collecting Victorian relics, among other things. There was not a nook of the large frame house that did not shelter objects of interest. Every one had a story, and Maggie Brownstone, Faye's mother, knew the story and could tell it with vivacity and charm.

In this environment Faye grew up. "No," she told me, "business was not my first career choice. As a teen-aged girl I wanted to be a dress designer. I would have taken a course in home economics at the university, but for financial and other, personal, reasons I couldn't. Because I had to earn a living I took a secretarial and bookkeeping course. Jobs were scarce, and without a profession or business training the future was bleak."

How did she get into the work she is doing now?

"By accident, believe me, and not by design! I've always been interested in and aware of antiques and art because, as you know, my mother and father had collected antiques for years. In fact, as kids we were sometimes embarrassed by what we considered at the time to be clutter. Eventually my mother decided she would like to open an antique shop, partly, I suppose, because her house was overflowing and partly because she didn't have enough to keep her busy. Her children were all married and away from home, and she had a yen to go into business. She talked to me about it."

What was Faye's reaction to the idea?

"Well, my daughter had just started kindergarten, and I was tired of doing volunteer, organizational, and community work. I put in the capital that was needed, and mother put in the stock, and we opened a tiny shop together, right downtown. It was mostly fun and not taken too seriously by either one of us because we both had outside interests; this was just going to be one of them, like curling or lawn bowling. Besides, I had the responsibility of bringing up a young child. So our hours were at our convenience.

"But you know what happens. I am blessed with great drive and curiosity, so I began to do a considerable amount of reading to learn something of the background of the many interesting and heretofore unknown things we were running across. The more I learned, the more exciting it became, and the more knowledge I gained, the more I realized there was an endless world of new discoveries leading from one field to another in the realm of antiques. It was a natural step from there to enter into the world of art, first the kind of art associated with antiques, and from there into the Group of Seven and their contemporaries, and ultimately into contemporary and Eskimo art."

11

Faye Settler's first regular job had been as a stenographer, and she stayed with stenography until she married. Her husband is a successful businessman, a creative, inventive kind of person who is immensely proud of his wife's success in her work as she is of his. He is not above lending a hand in the shop, when he is free to do so and is needed, as her father has also done over the years. The family is enthusiastic about what is now a large, but still personal, and vastly interesting business.

"Yes," said Faye, "my work is extremely satisfying as you've probably guessed from what I have already said. I find my interests expanding and each new experience leads to yet another which I find more stimulating than the one before. In the art gallery, my association with art, artists, and clients has broadened my view and further developed my awareness of the world around me.

"Did you know that I have made three trips to the Arctic? And that I took George Swinton's course on Eskimo art? If I were only fifteen or twenty years younger! I would like to live among the Eskimo people for a while."

Faye Settler also sees herself as one of the lucky ones, and certainly she has been spared some of the problems of the other self-employed women who spoke or wrote to me. She, like Gladys Neale, is fortunate in having had the backing of an interested and supportive family.

Most women working in business, in trade and commerce, are dependent upon their jobs for their livelihood and often for the support of others: children, parents, dependent husbands. The great majority of those whose husbands are also working work to raise the level of their standard of living, or to keep it on an even keel as children are added to the family or the needs of children expand. Some, not the majority, become, like Faye Settler, involved because they need an outlet for their intelligence and their energy. A few almost belligerently told me that they were in business not because they had to be – their husbands would be glad to "support" them. They believe that their position makes them independent and more innovative, gives them a stronger voice in fighting for the rights of others because they do not have to be tied to a job they dislike or find unsatisfying, and because they do not have to be anxious about holding a job and so can say their say without fear of reprisal.

It was strange to me that the last group of women seemed to feel such a need, almost a compulsion, to defend themselves. Were they fighting a feeling of guilt within themselves? Were they responding to spoken and unspoken criticism by their families, their friends, their neighbours? Were they the object of reproof from their co-workers? I asked Joyce, like Olga a former pupil of mine, who is now living in Montreal. At thirty-two Joyce is one of this group of women. Her husband is a free-lancing and prosperous engineer with a large clientele. They have a beautiful home, a summer cottage, and an apartment in Florida. Joyce is a graduate in interior design. The secretarial job she is holding, in the office of a furniture wholesale house, is to my way of thinking routine and well below her capability, but she likes it, and she is very conscientious about it, as conscientious as – more than, she says – her co-workers who "need" their jobs.

Joyce was emphatic. "The answer to all your questions is YES. Yes, yes, and yes. People make me feel guilty all the time, and I don't like it. Especially when times get a little tough and jobs are harder to come by. You have no idea how many people, none of whose business it is, have asked me why I am working when I don't have to, and my husband is so well to do. Some of the old biddies, and young ones too, have had the unmitigated gall to inquire what my husband thinks of my working, and doesn't it interfere with my social life, et cetera, et cetera. You just wouldn't believe it in this day and age! Even my own mother, who should know better, has hinted in her gentle way that it might be better for the children – I have two – and for Bill, my husband, if I were home all day. I sometimes feel that I am taking bread out of the mouths of hungry orphans by depriving their mother of a job! I console myself with the fact that I employ a full-time housekeeper. We can afford to pay her well, so she has been with us for a couple of years. When I get down in the dumps about it, I remind myself that if I am taking bread out of the mouths of one widow and her orphans by holding my job, I am putting it into the mouths of another widow and her orphans by giving my housekeeper a good job. She is a lot better off than when she did day work at the minimum wage. If I sound bitter it is because I am, real bitter. Why should I not have the right to work at something I enjoy doing simply because my husband happens to be successful in his line of work? And why, for God's sake, do I have to apologize for it?"

Joyce had obviously been more than annoyed; she feels that she has been and is still being harassed. Maybe she is overreacting. She does not think so. "Why, oh why," she said passionately, "should I be penalized for working because my husband has an income? If I were an actress or a pop singer it would be perfectly all right for me to hold a job doing what I could do best. But because I work in an office what I am doing is considered almost immoral by my family and friends. What about a man, when the positions are reversed? Suppose I were the professional and my husband an office worker? Would he be criticized for working? Well, maybe, but he would be criticized for working at something that didn't bring in as much money as his wife earned. He'd be getting raked over the coals as a lazy chiseler if he weren't working at all. It is simply not fair."

She did not appreciate what she considered my being funny when I suggested that perhaps she should be putting herself in a position where she might be making as much money as her husband. She might then be getting criticism, but for different reasons and perhaps from different people. She might be called aggressive and ambitious and hard, but she would have a grudging kind of respect. Moreover, her working would then not be related to her husband's ability to support her in style.

"No doubt," she said, "you are giving this advice tongue-in-cheek. How do I go about making this fabulous kind of salary you are talking about? I'm over thirty. I've worked for this company for several years. I know my employers think I'm pretty good, but they don't think of me as doing anything else but what I am now doing – secretarial work. I can't – or maybe I don't want to – go out on the road selling, even if they would consider me for that kind of job, and they won't. If I went to another company I wouldn't be any further ahead; in fact, I'd be worse off than I am now because at least here I have established that I am a good secretary."

Joyce told me, not rudely but with feeling, that I had missed the point. All she really wanted was to be allowed to do what she liked to do and did well without reference to her husband and his ability to "provide for" or "support" her. She is right, of course.

Joyce was also right about who did what.

In 1974, of all clerical jobs in Canada, 73 per cent were filled by women. Of all sales jobs, 32 per cent were filled by women; of all service and recreation jobs, 51.4 per cent were filled by women. The figures were not likely to be very different in 1976 or 1977 or 1978. Of all women working, 35.4 per cent held clerical jobs, 10.1 per cent were in sales, and 18 per cent in service occupations.[5] In the sales jobs, women generally sold the smaller items: foods, women's and children's clothing, notions, china, cosmetics. Men sold the large items which often carried commissions in addition to salaries or wages: furniture, large household appliances such as washers, dryers, refrigerators, and stoves, carpeting, automobiles, and farm equipment. Women were beginning to make names for themselves in real estate sales, house rather than commercial properties.

14

An Ontario survey in 1973 showed substantially the same distribution of occupations for its women as did Canadian figures for 1974: 35 per cent of all women employees were in clerical jobs, 10.1 per cent in sales, 17.8 per cent in service jobs. Half of all service jobs in Ontario were held by women, although women constituted only 35 per cent of the total labour force; 72.4 per cent of all clerical jobs were filled by women.[6] That means that over a million women in Canada and nearly a half-million in Ontario alone are doing jobs in offices and stores not too different from Joyce's, Zetta's, Olga's. They represent far and away the largest group of women in business, and sad to say are often the most underpaid – certainly in comparison with their male counterparts.

It is not unusual for "women's jobs" to carry less pay than "men's jobs." Although almost all the provinces, the territories and the federal government have legislation making mandatory equal pay for equal work, the definition of equal work has generally been "the same or similar work in the same establishment." As many of my informants have told me, and as was very evident in the offices in which Zetta and Julie work, women are engaged in the lower-paid jobs; the men in the offices do not engage in work the same as or similar to Julie's. I am sure that there is not a man in Zetta's company doing the same kind of secretarial work as Zetta herself is doing. In establishments where the work is similar there is enough difference in title and assignment to justify in the minds of employers and male employees a differential in salary or wages. A Women's Bureau report in 1975 points out that the average pay of men in clerical work is 56.7 per cent higher than that of women.[7] An earlier report from Ontario gives the percentage difference as 60.[8] The earnings of men in sales jobs, of which close to 40 per cent are filled by women, exceed the earnings of women by a startling 167.9 per cent.

More alarming than the differential in pay itself is the fact that in spite of legislation and publicity aimed at reducing the differences and eliminating wage discrimination on the basis of sex, the gap seems to be widening, particularly in offices. In 70 per cent of office occupations surveyed by the Canada Department of Labour, the differential in pay had increased in the three-year interval from 1969 to 1972.[9] Wage and salary increases on a percentage basis will continue to aggravate the discrepancies as the lowest paid get less and the higher paid more in successive wage settlements.

My former student Olga, the part-time check-out clerk in a super-market, does not belong to a union though she works in an occupation that is gradually becoming unionized. Neither do any other of the employed women I have so far quoted. In the strange pecking order of women's work, Julie or a bank teller or a stenographer, euphemistically described as a secretary, consider themselves a cut above the "saleslady," whom Zetta's parents saw as being just one cut above domestic service. Though many of them come from working-class families or are married to working-class husbands, the thought of organizing as a union has not appealed or even occurred to many women I talked with. In any event, only a few of them – some retail clerks, some employees of large government-related corporations like the CNR – are members of unions or welfare organizations of any kind. Almost no employees of financial institutions or office workers in commercial enterprises are unionized. Indeed, only 6.9 per cent of women employed in the category described by Statistics Canada as *Trade* are union members. The men do not have a much better showing (8.4 per cent), trade, I assume, being the essence of free enterprise. In the category identified as *Finance, insurance and real estate,* only 0.9 per cent of the women and 1.7 per cent of the men are members of unions.[10]

M. Patricia Marchak made a survey of 307 white-collar workers in British Columbia in 1969. Half the people surveyed were union members. She wrote:

We found that unions as they are presently constituted are no help to most white collar women. . . . Contrary to the widespread notion that women are against unions, we found that women were more favourable than men. Thirty-six per cent of the non-union women, compared to 28 per cent of the men, believed that workers like themselves should belong to unions. Thirty-five per cent of the women as compared with 26 per cent of the men said that they were willing to join a union themselves. Forty-one per cent of the women as compared to 36 per cent of the men thought their wages would improve if they were unionized. The most favourable to unionization were those with low job control and low income, among whom women were over-represented.[11]

Among union members the situation was different. As might have been expected, members were more favourable to unions than non-members, but men members favoured union membership more strongly than women members, probably, Ms. Marchak suggests, because the unions are male oriented and male dominated. Twice as many of the men as the women surveyed had held union offices, and women workers tended to benefit less than men from the work of the unions. Union as well as non-union women suffered from the strongly traditional attitudes of many unions. In spite of pressure from within and without for change, there are indications that male union members still believe strongly that woman's place is in the home.[12]

It appears, therefore, that if women workers in business are to improve their economic condition through collective bargaining, they will have to initiate and carry through massive changes in male-oriented and male-dominated unions, or form independent unions of their own. There is hope that this change can take place in Marchak's finding that the better-paid and more autonomous white-collar workers among women favour union membership more strongly than the lower-paid workers. From them may come the leadership that will eventually make it possible for women in the less secure, more dispensable jobs to benefit from union membership. Moreover, the unionization of civil servants and their strong bargaining strength, coupled with the fact that government-employed professionals like doctors and engineers are not above unionization, may have an effect on the lowlier clerks and salespeople.

Neither Julie at her switchboard nor Olga at her check-out counter may think that she is making a major contribution to the Canadian economy. Like Zetta when she went back to work, Julie and Olga are concerned about doing a job and earning the money they need. If they can enjoy and receive personal satisfaction from the job, so much the better. They are, however, intrinsic and necessary components of the business community of Canada. The computers would blink and go blank without them; the financial system would grind to a shuddering halt; retail stores and wholesale businesses would close down. Chaos would reign. These women and the many thousands whom they symbolize are essential to the lives and well-being of all Canadians.

Yet they do not take part in the major decision making of the companies and institutions for which they work. I have before me a list of the directors and officers of Massey-Ferguson Limited for the year 1975. Not one of them was a woman. Of twenty-nine officers of Bell Canada, not one was a woman; of twenty-two directors, two were women, one the chairman and the other a member of the Social and Environmental Affairs Committee. Of sixteen nominees to the Board of Directors of Algoma Steel for 1975, not one was a woman. I could go on through the major Canadian corporations and would find that the picture varies little from one to another, with here and there the name of a prominent woman. Some of us remember the days when it would have been just as fashionable to have a Jewish name and the picture of a black man in the annual reports of major corporations.

The reasons for this sad situation? They are many and complex. They lie deep in the society from which we spring, in Julie's remark that her boy friend doesn't want her to work after she's married; in Olga's feeling that she is not good for anything more than a part-time job at a check-out counter; in the attitudes of many union members; in the whole structure of our social and economic system. To believe that the reason resides in men like the businessman and employer of female labour I am going to quote is an oversimplification, certainly, and many of the women who wrote to me and spoke with me claim never to have run into anyone like him. Many, on the other hand, have. I am afraid he is typical of one segment of employers.

John Leggatt is a big man, tall, broad, with a big voice and a big smile and an enveloping handshake. His manufacturing business in a western city employs women in the shop and women in the office, many women, some of whom have been with him all through the twenty years he and his father before him have operated the business; it has now gone public, but he is president, general manager, and in every way the boss. I talked with him in his private office, a cubbyhole with no pretensions, in the six- or eight-storey building that houses plant and offices.

"Girls," he said, "they come and they go. Girls in the office? Well, Miss Black has been with me more than fifteen years. She's a fixture here. I don't know what we'd do without her. But the others? They all look the same to me after a while. Their names are different, and I have lived through cashmere sweaters and peek-a-boo blouses or whatever you call them." His laugh boomed out. "You won't believe it, but I kicked up one hell of a row when the first girl turned up in the office in a pant suit. I can't remember now why, because the girls in the shop have always worn slacks to work. Well, anyway, as you can see they wear what they damn well please now and I haven't a word to say about it. If the work is okay, they stay, whatever they wear; if they make a mess of things, they go."

He did not add that they came and went cheaply, but I am sure that is part of his rationale in employing them.

All this employer's middle-management people are men. He never starts a young man in the kind of job his women employees do. "For one thing," he told me in all innocence, "the boys wouldn't stick it. Girls are good at detail work. You women do that so well. You're finicky. . . . No, no, I mean that as a compliment. Being finicky is good for ordinary office work. Give me a good girl any day. She'll work rings around a boy at that kind of work."

18

Had he ever tried one of his "good girls" in the boys' jobs? "No, I can't say that I have. None of them has ever asked, and besides it's not for them. Come on, now, you know what happens. She'd meet a nice young man, get married, and have a baby within the year. No use training her, even if she could do it or wanted to do it."

Miss Black, I pointed out, had been with him for fifteen years or more. The company couldn't get along without her. Had he asked her? His laugh boomed again. "Her? Miss Black? Oh, come on. The only job good enough for her would be mine!"

When I said something to the effect that maybe he was right at that, he looked at me over his glasses in a kindly, condescending, unembarrassed way and said, "Well, now, my dear [I am at least ten and maybe fifteen years older than he is, but he might have been talking to a child], well, now, my dear, not all women want to be career women, and not all women are as smart as you are. [I had the feeling that he did not think I was at all smart.] It's all right for you to argue about women's place in business, but I must tell you that I prefer my wife – and my daughters – I have three of them, two happily married – I prefer them to be at home where they belong. Oh, of course, there are women who can do men's work, but frankly I don't like them."

This man is quite ready to admit the important role women play in offices and stores and wherever business is carried on, and he uses them to the utmost in his own business. He is kind to them in his fashion. He gives bonuses at Christmastime, as he told me with pride, and he pays for and attends staff picnics every summer, providing buses to carry his employees and their families to the picnic site and laying on huge quantities of buns, hot dogs, and mustard. He will not be happy, if he reads this description of himself, to see himself written about as a direct descendant of the benevolent slaveholder. And maybe the comparison is not fair. After all, there are no slaves today; his women employees are free to leave, and he will not raise a finger to keep them.

No, he is not the reason why women occupy the lowest levels of the business community. But he is one reason.

2

Women at Work, Then and Now

When I first knew her, Mrs. Provenski could not have been much more than forty years old, but she was already bent and gnarled. Her face was brown and wrinkled, with gaps and snags in the gums that showed when she smiled. As late as the middle 1930s she was our favourite, indeed our only, supplier of eggs and cottage cheese. She carried her bundles of cheese, her jars of sour cream, her pails of eggs three-quarters of a mile to the highway where she stood waiting patiently to catch the bus into the city. She had her regular customers to whose homes she trudged, laden with her eggs and dairy produce.

Mrs. Provenski was a good businesswoman; her trading kept her family from "relief" in the terrible thirties. And she did more than maintain a subsistence level. She saw to it that her sons stayed in high school and reached Normal School or business college. Before she died, long before her threescore years and ten, they had made a moderate success in real estate and were living in a style that their mother had never seen, even in the homes of her regular customers. Kerchiefed, bowed with work in the fields, speaking a barely intelligible, sadly battered English, shrewd, stubborn, Mrs. Provenski had a host of colleagues across the country from the time the first vegetables were grown on the first farms, the first cattle milked for their warm and frothy gift to the early settlers. In the early days of New France the wives of the first farmers must have brought their farm produce, as women have done from time immemorial, and sold it in stalls in the marketplace. Farm women have traditionally been, like Mrs. Provenski, small businesswomen, keeping for their own use and for their homes and their children the "egg money" and often the "milk money" in the days before mass marketing of farm commodities.

The story of businesswomen goes back a long way in Canada, for even before the forerunners of Mrs. Provenski had produce to sell, there were Frenchwomen like Jeanne Mance and Marguerite Bourgeoys. Micheline D.-Johnson, writing in 1968, had this to say:

What is exceptional in the case of New France is the unusually large number of women who played significant roles in laying the spiritual and material foundations of the colony. Indeed what leaves the contemporary historian impressed above all on reading the numerous documents left behind by these women is not so much their piety and devotion as their immense dynamism and determination. Not only did the Ursulines and the Hospitalières finance their own enterprises, but their capital was raised in France also by women. The owners of seigniories, they knew how to exploit their lands wisely, and their writings reveal them as fully conscious of the economic problems that beset the colonies.[1]

As settlement spread and the vast spaces of the North and West lured men with promises of gold and grain, women came with and after them. Just as women sold the produce of the farms, they were soon providing food and shelter for pay wherever new settlements sprang up. The "boarding house" was a fixture of every little town too small to have a hotel and in larger towns was used to accommodate those visitors who stayed too long to afford the hotel prices, or who preferred the more homelike atmosphere of a boarding house. D'Arcy McGee, who had the dubious honour of being the first Canadian to suffer political assassination, in 1868 died on the steps of Mrs. Trotter's boarding house in Ottawa where he was living. Many a more fortunate parliamentarian has spent months of every year in a boarding house while the House of Commons was in session. It still provides cheaper and less lonely accommodation than a hotel or a furnished apartment.

During the early part of the twentieth century, the ubiquitous commercial traveller used the boarding houses almost exclusively. My father was a travelling salesman for a couple of years when we lived in a small town in western Manitoba, and my mother was alone at home with two young children while he was on the road. One night, about one o'clock, just after the CN Flyer had passed through, my mother was awakened by a loud banging on the front door of the isolated house in which we lived. Thinking that my father had come home earlier than he had expected, and that, as was not unusual, he had forgotten his key, she ran downstairs in nightgown and bare feet to let him in. Imagine her dismay and terror when she saw a tall fur-capped stranger standing in the doorway. "Let me in," he said brusquely. "I am going to stay a couple of nights." Then he must have seen the look of fright on her blanched face. "Oh, pardon me," he said, raising his cap, "I thought this was still a boarding house. I always stayed here."

And he backed hurriedly away, leaving my poor mother so shaken she could hardly stumble up the steep stairs to her little girls, whom she had already seen in her mind's eye slaughtered in their beds.

My father heard the story from her, and later again and again as he crisscrossed his territory on the CNR. The tall fur-capped commercial traveller thought it a great joke that he had "frightened a little woman almost out of her wits" one chilly November night.

The women who operated the boarding houses (in 1931, 1,555 women in Manitoba alone were identified as "Boarding and Lodging Housekeepers"[2]) were not easily frightened. Many of them ran their places with an iron hand, dealt with transients and regulars, and occasionally – only occasionally – developed their boarding houses into small and flourishing hotels. And some ran very profitable houses, without boarding privileges, renting their space by the quarter-hour and half-hour and hour in frontier settlements where women were few and men outnumbered them fifty and a hundred to one.

Other women were like Martha Louise Purdy, later Martha Louise Black, who followed the gold rush to Dawson City, was abandoned by her husband, had a baby alone in a cabin in 1898, and founded a sawmill. She lived to remarry and become the wife of the commissioner of the Yukon. A businesswoman with dash.

In the days when I was growing up, the small store was a feature of every corner in our residential neighbourhood. It sold meat, groceries, and "confectionery" or "dry goods" – yard goods, small items of apparel, children's clothing, and sundries: elastic by the yard, hooks and eyes, buttons, thread. Most of these little stores were family enterprises in which husband and wife worked side by side, the wife usually being responsible not only for over-the-counter sales and consultation but for keeping the books and watching over the accounts that regular customers were allowed to carry, sometimes in amounts running into hundreds of dollars, sometimes merely credit extended from payday to payday. In the "general stores" that served every town and village women also worked side by side with their husbands until the establishments grew large enough and profitable enough to be able to afford hired help, both male and female.

A friend of my family who would be well over a hundred years old if she were still living worked with her husband in their general store for most of their lives together. In the late 1890s she had come to Canada from middle Europe, a young wife with two babies. The ship on which she had come had lain in quarantine in Boston for three weeks before the tired, hungry, bewildered immigrants in the steerage were allowed to land. She never forgot the hot, exhausting, utterly fascinating journey across half a continent in creaking wooden colonist cars, or the kindness of the women who helped her when her babies were trainsick and she herself unbelievably homesick. Idealistically her husband, who had hitherto never stuck a seed in the ground, had planned on becoming a farmer, but flood, drought, and sheer inexperience had killed that dream. They settled finally after two years of hopeless struggle in a small prairie town, part French, part newly arrived Mennonite, part Scottish. With her third child on the way and no resources but her own ingenuity and the love and support of her husband she made a home in that bleak little town. She tended a large garden, raised a large family, two or three times a week drove a horse and buggy into the city twenty-five miles away, crossing the river on a ferry, to sell produce and to buy supplies for the house and the store, and was as knowledgeable about the business as her husband and later her sons. She was an unusual person in that she lived into her nineties in an age when women died young, but in her energy and business ability she was the norm rather than the exception for women of her time and place in Canadian history.

Margaret Brown was a little younger and from a different culture. Her family was among the earliest of the British settlers at the forks of the Red and the Assiniboine rivers, her father one of the first aldermen of the newly formed city of Winnipeg in the 1870s. I watched Margaret, who forty-five years ago was to me an elderly woman, typing with four fingers, as she had been taught at her business school, rapidly and as accurately as the typists whose fingers now fly over the keyboards of electric typewriters. She had worked in an office prior to her marriage in the early 1900s and had always maintained her typing skills; she had ambitions as a writer and every now and then sold a story to a newspaper's magazine section or to a Canadian magazine. Her major interest was local history, and she wrote about it with interest and passion.

Women, says Sylva Gelber, head of the Women's Bureau of the federal Department of Labour, have been in offices as long as there have been offices in Canada. Margaret was one of the first, a pretty young woman in a high boned collar, a skirt tightly pinched in at the waist, and high boots under a frilled petticoat that showed when she lifted her long skirt above the sticky Manitoba gumbo. In the spring, and whenever it rained, the mile or so she walked to work from the old house that had once been a homestead to downtown Winnipeg seemed a lot longer and wetter than it is now.

A Winnipeg school is named for Margaret Scott, and for many years the Margaret Scott nursing mission served the needs of Winnipeg's newly arrived immigrants, Winnipeg's poor and distressed. The woman who was so honoured was born in Ontario in 1855, of Huguenot and United Empire Loyalist stock, her father a judge of the Ontario County court. Orphaned at twelve and raised by her aunts, Margaret Rutten Boucher married a Peterborough lawyer, William Hepburn Scott. By twenty-five she was a destitute widow who had to find some way of making a living. Edith Paterson wrote of her: "Few women were employed in offices in those days, but she got a job with the Midland Railway and earned $25 a month. When Midland amalgamated with the Grand Trunk Railway she was transferred to the audit office in Montreal, in charge of a large number of girls. There she worked too hard and had a breakdown."[3]

She was advised to leave the murky East for the "bracing climate of the West" and came to Winnipeg. There she found that her lack of shorthand was a handicap. "Unfortunately the only person teaching it at this time was W. F. Perkins, the court stenographer. But for some inexplicable reason he objected to teaching it to a woman." Mrs. Scott, however, was lucky. When a gentleman named F. W. Heuback heard of the refusal he offered to teach her shorthand, free of charge. She became a proficient stenographer. Later Mrs. Scott left business for good works, particularly with disadvantaged women and children, but her early career must not have been very different from that of many women who were forced by economic circumstances to find a way of earning a living.

Undoubtedly many of the first women office workers were "ladies"; office work, poorly paid as it was and low in status, still ranked higher in the social scale than being a "saleslady," a distinction that seems to have been retained to the present day. Margaret Brown and Margaret Scott were a generation apart in age, and several generations away from the young women now entering the world of work, but their problems do not seem to have been much different, nor their satisfactions.

Although women were working in offices by 1880, in statistical tables from 1881 to 1921 the categories of "stenographer" and "typist" do not appear in lists of occupations favoured by women ten years old and over. (The lower age limit in itself tells something about the conditions of employment in this country during the latter part of the nineteenth and the beginning of the twentieth centuries.) The categories of employment in which sizable numbers of women were employed in Canada in 1891, for example, were servants, 35.4 per cent; dressmakers and seamstresses, 16.8 per cent; teachers, 7.5 per cent; farmers – general, 5.9 per cent; wholesale and retail proprietors, managers, superintendents, 3.9 per cent. By 1901, saleswomen in wholesale and retail trades had been added to the categories, with a total of 2,729 out of 237,949 women employed, or just over 1 per cent. Statistics for 1921 show that by that time teaching was absorbing close to 10 per cent of the female work force; and while domestic service, though still the leading category with 88,825 out of a total work force of 490,150, had fallen to about 18 per cent, wholesale and retail saleswomen now comprised 7.3 per cent of all women working outside the home – the third largest group.[4]

Women, whose employment had been accelerated by the shortage of manpower during the First World War, were now in the business world, in offices and stores, and were there to stay, although with some fluctuations of numbers. These swelled during times of depression, when women sought jobs in order to supplement or replace the wages of husbands who were unemployed, to support themselves, and to provide support for parents, sisters, and brothers. During the dreadful thirties their wages sank to unbelievably low levels as, unorganized and desperate, they took whatever work was available, often working as domestic servants for miserable shelter and scanty board.

Not only were women established in the business world, but their status and their subordinate roles were also firmly established and destined to remain relatively unchanged for decades to come. The figures for 1921 show that the percentage of female wholesale and retail proprietors, managers, and superintendents had dropped from a slender enough 3.9 per cent in 1911 to 1.4 per cent.

Moreover, a table comparing average earnings in 1931 of women and men gives an average weekly wage of $17.43 for female stenographers and typists and no corresponding wage for males, although "Bookkeepers, Cashiers, female," earned an average of $17.25 a week as compared with $25.97 for "Bookkeepers, Cashiers, male." "Other Clerical (Office Clerks), female," were being paid an average of $16.87 as compared with $24.00 for males. The *Canada Yearbook* for 1959 shows that average weekly earnings of office workers in the last week of October 1957 were men, $81.08; women, $50.80.[5] In spite of human rights and equal-pay legislation, the differential for work of equal value has not been substantially reduced. Women workers in business have remained true to their history.

Rita Sloan Tilton, addressing herself to her secretarial colleagues in 1974, has this to say:

A look into yesterday brings us to a startling revelation. Your good friend (and mine), the typewriter, introduced women to the then predominant world of business in the late 1880s. Closely associated with the use of the

25

typewriter in the office was the introduction and acceptance of shorthand as a communication tool. This marriage of the typewriter and shorthand played an important role in the emergence of the position of secretary. Although men filled a number of secretarial positions, work involving shorthand and typewriting soon became accepted as women's work.[6]

It is hard to understand why Ms. Tilton considered women's takeover of routine office work a startling revelation. It seems a natural development. The work did not require physical strength; nor, in the minds of employers, did it require much training or preparation. The pay was hardly such as to attract men who had families to raise or who had ambitions for greater things.

When literacy was still a rarity and the wielder of the pen had about him an aura of magic, clerical work was still man's work, although the men who did it, being only writers and transcribers, did not have the status of the true male: the fighter and the striver. When spreading literacy took the magic out of writing, the status of the clerk declined still further. Shorthand and typing, as Ms. Tilton indicates, made clerical work completely accessible to women. Widespread literacy took it finally out of the hands of scholars and put it first into the hands of the Bob Cratchits among men and eventually almost totally into the hands of women.

The new technologies have increased rather than decreased the number of people in white-collar jobs as machines and computers have taken over the work that was once done by hand. Whole new vistas of employment have therefore opened for women in offices, particularly in fields like communication and information storage and retrieval. Business schools and community colleges in their business departments offer courses ranging from the preparation of data processing cards to three and four levels of Data Processing Programming and Data Processing Mathematics. The content of Data Processing Programming III, for example, is described in a community college calendar as follows: "The programming languages FORTRAN and RPG will be studied. Problems will be studied. Problems utilizing pertinent features of these two languages will be solved."

It is apparent, then, that in spite of the low pay and low status of clerical work, some of the jobs, especially those of a secretarial or accounting nature and in some sales occupations, require something more than bare literacy.

While 24.8 per cent of the total female population has Grade 8 standing or less, only 17.4 per cent of working women are so poorly

educated.[7] In the total population more women than men have attended high school, 55.2 per cent to 49.9 per cent, as of 1972. In the labour force the ratio is 58.6 to 51.1 per cent. Although fewer women than men have some university education, a higher percentage of the university-trained women is working; only 7.3 per cent of the total female population has gone to university, but 10.5 per cent of all employed women has had some university education. Highly educated women, then, are more likely to be in the labour force than poorly educated women. An information sheet issued by the Ontario Women's Bureau bears out this conclusion. One-fourth of Ontario's women with less than Grade 5 education worked outside the home in 1971, whereas 63 per cent of Ontario's female university graduates were employed.[8]

The replies I received from ninety women who wrote in response to the questionnaire I had sent them, and who described themselves as being "in the business world," provided further corroboration if that is necessary. Only four – my correspondents ranged in age from twenty-two to seventy-one – had had less than high school education; twenty-one held at least one university degree; sixty-five had completed high school. Eight had post-secondary training of some kind other than university courses related to their jobs: in accountancy, insurance, real estate.

Where do they come from, these women in business? From every segment of society, from town and city and farm; from every social and economic level; from every ethnic grouping. They would be representative of the general population of women were it not for several probably predictable but interesting exceptions.

One has already been noted: the educational level is somewhat above that of the general population. The age distribution of women at work is also somewhat different from that of the total female population. As might be expected, the restraints of marriage and child-bearing, among other influences, develop age patterns for working women that differ from the age patterns of working men and from those of the whole range of women.

Women in the labour force in 1974 were generally somewhat younger than their male counterparts: 33.8 per cent of women were in the age group fourteen to twenty-four as compared with 24.5 per cent of men, while 24.1 per cent of the women not in the labour force fell into this age grouping as compared with 42.8 per cent of the men. Over half the unemployed women – that is, those actively looking for employment – were also within this decade.[9] Girls go out to work earlier in those

regions of Canada where economic conditions are least favourable and where school systems tend to make less provision for the needs of a variety of students. The Atlantic region sends a higher proportion of its girls to work between fourteen and twenty-four (43 per cent of the female labour force is under twenty-five) than does Ontario or British Columbia (30.5 and 32.9 per cent respectively).[10] For the rest of their working lives the distribution of age among working men and working women is not significantly different.

Maggie Henderson belongs to what is currently a tiny segment of women in business. She is a Saulteaux Indian. She had an unhappy beginning in a one-room school in a small town near the reserve where she was born, so unhappy that her father was determined that she should have a better chance. He sent her to live with her mother's sister in the city, where she spent almost three years "crying inside myself," as she told me. But she made it to high school, where she took a business course. Maggie is a good-looking woman, well built, smartly dressed, and soft spoken. She should have had no trouble finding a job, with her good school references.

"By some strange coincidence," she said, "the jobs were always filled just before I got there. In a couple of cases my letters of application brought a telephone call asking me to come in for an interview, but once I showed up I saw that closed look on the face of the fellow who was doing the interviewing. Finally one company offered me a job filing on a trial basis. I was so scared I nearly messed everything up. It was a good thing the trial period was for two weeks because the first week I was too scared even to ask anyone for help, and no one volunteered. Then I got up the nerve to ask one of the other girls and found that she was shy too. I was Indian, and she had never met an Indian woman before and didn't know how to talk to me. We became good friends, and she helped me a lot. Anyway, I was lucky because about that time employers were beginning to become self-conscious about both women and native people. Or maybe I wasn't so lucky. I became the office showpiece. I was terribly uncomfortable because I was obviously being pointed out to visitors and customers as if I were some kind of curiosity. There were times when I was ready not only to quit but to blow up and quit. I didn't do either. I just gritted my teeth and made up my mind that I would show them that I was a human being and not a monkey in a cage. Finally someone offered me a better job, and then a better one. I've changed jobs several times, and always because someone wanted me. I suppose I am still a token sort of person; we Indian people

are sadly underrepresented in the white-collar jobs. But we're getting there. You know what? The women are giving the leadership. We have the drive, and we have the tongues. We do the talking, and we are pulling ourselves up and out. If making it in the white man's world is a good thing, it's we women who'll be doing it. I'm just not always sure it is the best thing for us, maybe just the only thing."

Anyway, Maggie says things are getting better. "Schooling first, and then confidence," she says, "not to mention a big educational campaign directed at employers. We have to fight on two fronts: ourselves and the rest of the world. It's tough, but not impossible. I'm not a militant, but there are times!"

Maggie is not married and is fiercely determined not to be. "I've seen what happened to my sisters and to my aunt. They're bogged down. I'm not going to be. I'm sending money home now and helping out the younger ones in the family; I have a young sister and a niece living with me. I'm not making all that much money, but I have enough to set them an example. They're getting a better education and a better chance than I had."

The older among us remember the days before human rights and equal opportunity legislation, days when Maggie's problems, perhaps in smaller measure, were the problems of many segments of the population. In the 1930s Rose, who is tall, blonde, and Nordic in appearance, if I may use that ill-fated adjective, worked for five years in the office of a company that would never have hired her if its officers had known that she was Jewish and would not have kept her on the job if they had discovered the fact. This was in a city that prided itself on its cosmopolitan nature, in a company that served a cosmopolitan population, and never would it have admitted its hiring policy publicly. Rose, however, knew the policy and suffered the indignity of listening to her bosses' carelessly anti-Semitic conversation, just as I am sure Maggie still suffers the indignity of comments regarding the Indian people. Rose suffered because jobs were scarce; she had to eat, and she had to contribute to her family's support. So for five long years she lived a lie, until the time came when she could leave the horror – and horror it was – behind her. She did not even have the comfort, or discomfort, of being a token.

Few studies that I am aware of have been made in Canada on the subject of ethnicity as it affects women in business. John Porter's *The Vertical Mosaic* did touch on the subject.[11] He pointed out that certain ethnic groups prior to 1965 were overrepresented in some occupations and underrepresented in others and saw little change in the pattern of representation between 1931 and 1961, a period during which one might have expected drastic changes. In the clerical occupations, Jewish, Irish, English, and Scottish women were overrepresented as a percentage of their total numbers in the work force while French, Chinese, Eastern and other Central European, Japanese, and native Indian women were all underrepresented. The reasons for the over- and underrepresentation are related to other factors than bias in favour of or against them, although that undoubtedly existed. The level of education, family and ethnic perceptions of women's responsibilities and roles, the distribution of these groups between urban and rural residence, and the aspirations of women as governed by these factors must surely have contributed to the situation.

My guess would be that the representation of these groups in white-collar jobs is considerably changed in the 1970s, especially for groups like the Japanese, whose forced diaspora during the Second World War and after changed their status from rural to urban. Immigration patterns during the intervening years have produced different sets of disadvantaged populations, unfortunately leaving Maggie's people still close to the minimum of representation in white-collar jobs, although as Maggie said to me, "Things *are* getting better!"

The position of women in Quebec merits a book in its own right. All I can hope to do is to pass on the opinions of a few Québécoises. Like that of the woman who replied to a question asking why women might be at a disadvantage in business, "Because ALL Quebec men are male chauvinist pigs!!! I mean it." And the more reasoned but no less impassioned analysis of the situation given me by Lucille Caron of the Women's Bureau, federal Department of Labour. Ms. Caron is a Quebecker by birth now living in Ottawa. There are indicators of social change, she says. Legislation is a major one. Quebec was the first province to establish an advisory council on the status of women, by an act of the National Assembly. Traditionally, she reminded me, Quebec has been a closed community in order to survive and so has built up a self-defence mechanism to maintain its culture and traditions. Women in Quebec are not dominant in terms of the law; the husband is the unconditional head of the family, at least in law.

Yet from the practical point of view, she says, the general pattern has been the glorification of the mother. The absence of the father's concern in the day-to-day life of the family has been a strong fact of life. Historically and culturally the mother was entirely responsible for the home and children. The mother image was very important and prominent in religion as in practice, and generations of Quebeckers were brought up under her influence. Male "superiority" may be a counteraction. Interpretation of the influential doctrines of St. Paul and of St. Thomas Aquinas as mistrust of the feminine should not be underestimated either. From all these things stemmed male discomfort in the presence of women in equalizing situations (and the feeling of my correspondent that all men are male chauvinists).

Lucille Caron made the comment that women were permitted by their men to be servants or saints or sinners. There was no room for women as human beings. Nuns were respected because of the religious connotations and because they were non-threatening.

But Quebec women are not backward in awareness. Mass communication has contributed to it, as has the educational break with the church.

I spoke with other Quebec women who reinforced much of what Ms. Caron had said to me. They too believed that more Quebec women are learning to think of themselves as having roles outside those of wife and mother. Marguerite, a Montrealer, told me about her mother who at forty-eight decided that she was going to get herself a job. She was tired of asking her husband for every penny she needed to run the household and to look after her personal needs. Her five children were well on their way to independence, and, she said, if they weren't, they should be.

So Marguerite's mother enrolled at Dawson College and took a business course. She paid for it with the money she had been secretly saving from the housekeeping allowance – "You'd be surprised at how many women accumulate a little nest egg . . . not exactly stealing from the husbands, just not telling them about it" – and got herself a job in the office of a biscuit-manufacturing company. She loves her work, loves the money she earns, has taken a vacation for the first time in her life, and feels like a new woman.

How did her husband react to all this? Well, he yelled a lot for a while, then he sulked, and now he boasts to the boys at the pub about what a smart wife he has. He says he won't touch her money, but he hasn't complained too much about the new furniture in the living room, either.

So the winds of change are blowing, in Quebec as elsewhere.

As more married women continue to work after marriage, or return to work soon after they have had their children, single women have gradually been losing their pre-eminence in the female work force. In

1964, 24.6 per cent of the female population was single; in 1974 that proportion had risen only slightly to 25.9 per cent. The proportion in the female labour force, however, had changed dramatically; it had shrunk from 39.0 per cent in 1964 to 33.8 per cent in 1974.[12] The group is atypical also in the fact that its members constitute a relatively high proportion of the women aged twenty-four to thirty-four, since those are the years when married women tend to withdraw from work to raise their childen. But more of the single women later.

How do women get into business?

They tell me that they do not have as many avenues open to them as men do.

Many girls, like many boys, are working at least part time before they leave school, although generally it is harder for them to get part-time jobs and summer work than it is for boys. Government-sponsored programs for students help, but even in those the young women students I spoke to believed that their male classmates received more encouragement and more consideration. "Nothing overt, you understand," one of my former students said to me, "but somehow the boys seem to get into the higher-paid jobs."

As for the jobs they are able to find for themselves, "Well, I did baby-sitting at twenty-five cents an hour," one of my contemporaries said to me, "while the boys were able to work on the highways or the railways and make anywhere from two to four dollars an hour, a lot of money in those days. My granddaughter is having identical problems today though the actual amounts are different."

"My introduction to business," a woman in the hotel and restaurant field told me, "was as a car-hop. I got the job on my own when I was fourteen. I must confess that I wasn't honest about it. I needed my principal's and my parents' signatures on the work permit, and I knew they wouldn't sign, so I got two different friends to write fancy signatures for me. I was on the job for a week before my family discovered that I was working and what I was doing. They were worried because I was so tired, didn't want to eat anything, and fell into bed at nine o'clock dead beat. Well, they were good sports about it when I finally told them what I was doing – I didn't tell them about the forgeries. They let me stay on. I went on and finished school and worked in an office for a couple of years, but I guess I must have liked dishing out food. I talked my way into a manager's job in a small restaurant on the highway near the edge of town, and got into the business legitimately. Then I married the boss."

Waiting on table at holiday resorts provided the first work for several of the women I talked with; tutoring students for summer school examinations was another small source of income. "A thankless job," said the secretary of a newspaper publisher in a small eastern city, "with terrible pay. It served one purpose. It convinced me I didn't want to be a teacher."

"I dipped chocolates for two months one summer," another woman told me. "How that chocolate ever hardened I'll never know because I am sure the room we worked in was almost as hot as the chocolate boiling in the vat."

A number of women who work in department stores or elsewhere in the retail trade followed in their mothers' footsteps. Mother had worked full or part time behind the counter, and when daughter reached working age, at fifteen or sixteen, she gravitated to holiday work in the store and then to full-time work on leaving school.

Many of the younger women simply completed a business course at high school, private business school, or community college, applied for a job, and got it. One of my former pupils who works in a trust company office asked, "Was it really that hard to get a job in the olden days? I sure get tired of hearing how lucky I am to get such a good job right out of school. We've two old ladies in the office who are always warning us that times are getting tough, and jobs don't grow on trees."

I assured her, though I am not convinced that she really believed me, that it really was that hard to get a job in the olden days and that in some parts of the country and in some industries it is still pretty hard.

Women tend to stay on their jobs. There is a bit of shifting around, as there is with young men, during the early years in the labour force until they find something in which they are comfortable or to which they are suited, followed in many cases by a break for child-bearing and then a return to something that is permanent. A significant number of single women among my correspondents, now in their forties, had worked for only one or two employers throughout their careers. The picture of employment that emerges, from statistics and from conversations with businesswomen, seems to reconcile the comment of people like my employer friend who claims that his "girls" come and go before he gets to know them, and the seemingly contradictory comment of one of my correspondents that women do not change jobs often enough. "The only way for a woman to attain upward mobility," she wrote, "is to change employers frequently. If you started out as a stenographer or clerk, you'll never make it with that company because your employer is never able to think of you as promotable. So move, bettering yourself every time you do."

The statistics say that very few women are self-employed, no more than 4 per cent. Among the women I used as a source of information the percentage is much higher. A few had been self-employed at one time or another and had returned to a job; some were employed in a family business or operated their own businesses or were independent single operators: in personnel work, accounting, real estate sales. By far the majority said they were interested in being self-employed, believing that they would have a better opportunity for self-development or advancement in their chosen field if they were on their own. Without exception the self-employed women with whom I spoke or corresponded were enthusiastic about their careers, which were varied: several owners of tourist lodges from Prince Edward Island to Vancouver Island, a film exhibitor, accountants, restaurateurs, proprietors of dress shops, florists, to name a small sampling.

Two or three had inherited, or inherited a share in, a family business and had continued it. Some had begun at home.

Often the heads of families, with small children to care for, with day care financially inaccessible even when available, and with their only security in the house they live in, women have looked about them for the kinds of business they could conduct from the home base within hours that are convenient for them.

Lillian was one of several women who ruefully recounted her first attempts at door-to-door selling. She tried cosmetics. Others "were into" encyclopaedias, kitchenware, spices, and a variety of other household goods and products. "I had done canvassing for various charities before my husband took sick and had to quit his job. You know, the community club, the Red Cross, and things like that. I thought I was pretty good at approaching people and that I had a tough hide. I could take being turned down. Well, it was one thing to be turned down for a donation to the community club. It's different when you walk your feet off hour after hour and don't make a single sale, even when people are polite to you, which isn't often. I went the coffee party route, too, inviting my friends and having a demonstration of something or other. I felt like a heel, although I honestly believed in the product I was selling. After all, I was putting my friends on the spot. In the end, I was stuck with a lot of stuff I couldn't sell. I wasn't smart enough to read the fine print in the agreement or to ask for legal advice. I was just enthusiastic – and desperate."

Lillian can laugh at her experiences now. She sells insurance, successfully, and believes that she learned a great deal from her door-to-door selling of cosmetics.

Edith was more successful in her home enterprise. She began by doing what she had been trained to do: typing manuscripts, especially theses and technical papers. She lives in an industrial city that is also a university centre. Her work was of top quality, and she was soon receiving more jobs than she could handle. She has been in business for twelve years and currently employs from five to ten women, depending on the time of year and the demand. She has expanded into duplicating and recently into providing research assistance for the preparation of papers. Some time ago the business became too big for a home operation, and she now rents an office and work room not far from the university, has a capital investment in office equipment, and a flourishing business.

It all began in her spare room at home. "Absolutely fascinating," she says. "You have no idea how much I have learned and the wonderful people I meet and work with. I was left all alone when my husband died, absolutely alone in that city without even the money to pick myself up and leave. The house was mortgaged; we hadn't been able to afford much insurance. Who would have thought that he would die suddenly and leave me high and dry? It was a struggle. The first year almost killed me, especially since I couldn't let my two boys see how desperate I was. I didn't know many people. The only things I could do well were to keep house and to type. So I typed."

Which brings me to the problem of the female head of family. Again and again, as I spoke with and read the stories of women in business, that problem came to the fore. Edith appears in Statistics Canada listings under the caption "Other," that is, widowed, divorced, or separated, a category that in 1974 represented 12.2 per cent of women in the total population, and 9.1 per cent of women in the labour force, somewhat fewer than the 9.9 per cent in 1964.[13] In 1971 in all Canada there were an estimated 338,000 single-parent families, of which 85 per cent were headed by women. Although families with female heads made up only 7 per cent of all Canadian families, they formed 20 per cent of all Canadian low-income families. Forty-four per cent of all Canadian families without fathers in the home were classified as low income, whereas only 14 per cent of all families headed by males were considered poor. The median income of single-parent families headed by women was just over half that of similar families headed by men.

But these are statistics. Edith is a real person. So is Colleen. Colleen is thirty-four years old. She wrote to me at considerable length, "during the middle of the night," she said, and from the heart:

I feel I fall into a special category of women who have been overlooked in the overall picture of women in employment.

I was deserted ten years ago, left with three boys, aged one, two, and three. I went looking for work and took the first job I could get, having had very little business experience. I have spent these years hanging on to jobs I was not happy with but terrified to give up because they offered security. I have not been able to upgrade myself educationally because I just did not have the stamina to carry a heavier load than I was carrying. I have resented this, because I would like to be in a position to earn more money, not for luxuries but for the necessities. Maybe I shouldn't complain. I now have ten years' work experience, so my income is finally above poverty level, and we manage, with care, on my salary. But what about the hundreds of other women who do not have the experience and qualifications for a half decent paying job? This concerns me very much.

Colleen had her troubles finding a job that paid enough to make her independent. She could, she wrote, have gone on welfare, because she had absolutely no money, but she would have felt disgraced. So she went job hunting.

Employers, she found, have a strange attitude towards sole-support mothers. "They are afraid you will stay home when your children are sick, etc. They don't seem to realize that when you are sole support you put your job first and your children second, because you have to support your children; there is no one else who will step in to help you financially. So you make terrific sacrifices at the expense of your children just to hang on to that job. It takes a long time to prove to your employer that you are sincere in your efforts to give your best to him."

Perhaps because she is now more secure, or because she feels somewhat protected by human rights codes, Colleen believes that there has been an important change in attitude of management in this regard. Employers, she thinks, seem less reluctant now to hire sole-support mothers than they did ten years ago when she first set out to look for work.

She faced similar difficulties in getting accommodation. Another woman whom I questioned about this problem insists that the prejudice shown by landlords is not against sole-support mothers but against children, whether they are living with one parent or two. Colleen, however – young, wounded in her pride, and desperate – perceived her problems as those of a sole-support working mother. "My knees," she wrote, "are sore from begging for a job and a place to live just because I am divorced and have three children. Instead of checking on you for references both employers and landlords have had a tendency to say NO – automatically."

A much higher proportion of my correspondents were in the "Other" group – separated, divorced, widowed – than the statistics suggest: twenty-nine of the eighty-five women who answered the question about their marital status. Some expressed views similar to Colleen's. Most, however, had fought their way through to a successful, or at least satisfying, career in business, and felt – as Colleen did – that their children had suffered initially as a result of the loss of a father but had gained in responsibility and respect for their mother because of her work outside the home.

A few respondents claimed that their careers in business had contributed to the breakdown of their marriage: "My husband had a good job, but he couldn't bear it that I had reached the point where I was making more money than he was."

And "My husband and I moved apart. My interests were very different from his, and my job was taking more and more of my time and attention. When I was home all day I was able to concentrate on ways to please him. He was brought up in a household where his mother and his sisters had done everything for him, and I had started out that way, but not when I was at work every day, all day. After all, I was working as hard as he was and making as much money. I couldn't give him the service he was accustomed to."

In 1974 57.1 per cent of the women in the labour force were married; they represented 36.7 per cent of all married women. Ontario and the Prairie Provinces had the highest percentage of married women in the labour force, 61.7 and 59.0 per cent respectively, while Quebec had the lowest percentage, 49.9. Just over 51 per cent of all married women in the population aged twenty to twenty-four were working outside the home.[14] These are the years of "saving to pay off the mortgage" and "putting aside enough money so we can furnish the house," or buy a car, or a summer cottage, the years before the settling-down process. Over half the young married women stay on at work during their first years of marriage. Well over a third remain there through most of their lives.

Married women who thought of themselves as being successful in business frequently gave credit to the support and understanding of husbands and families. "I could never have done what I am doing, or enjoyed doing it, if my husband had not been right there encouraging me, telling me how good I was, etc."

"When I first went back to work it put a strain on my husband and family, and on me too because I was always worrying about what might be happening to the children when I couldn't be there at lunch time, and so on. But we worked out a plan that has been right for us. The schools have both my husband's telephone number and mine, and it is understood that whoever can get away most easily goes when there is an emergency. With five kids, all active, there have been several emergencies. Like the time Tim broke his leg in two places, and I was out of town on business, and the time the school nurse called us to pick up Janie because she had fallen on the playground and showed symptoms of concussion. My husband, as it happens, handled that one too."

On the other hand, most employed women seemed to accept without question their double workload, one outside the home, the other at home. They believe that it's natural for the wife and mother to do the household work.

"I am always home in time to make dinner."

"My husband does the outside work; I do the inside work. To tell you the truth I never thought of any other way."

"When I went back to work I organized my work so that I could get it done in the time I had, leaving free time to spend with my husband and family. It means getting up an hour earlier, making lunches and so on before I leave for work. But we manage very nicely, thank you."

What does father do when he comes home from work?

"Well, he likes a little rest before supper."

"He's very helpful, really. He carries in the groceries I pick up on my way home from work. But honestly, I get a lot more done if he reads the paper or watches the news on TV."

The part-time worker is an important segment of the female working population. In 1974 she represented over 25 per cent of the total of employed women, as compared with 18.8 per cent a dozen years earlier, so that she makes a substantial contribution to the Canadian economy.

Many of the part-time workers are like Olga, working in retail stores as cashiers, sales personnel, sorters, check-out clerks on a regular weekly basis. A few come in only on an emergency basis; they are called to help out during major sales, before long weekends, during the pre-Christmas rush, as relief workers during the vacation season. Almost all the women I spoke with who are in the first category work because they need the money, although many added that they also like to get out of the house.

"It makes for a break in the routine."

"It's good to get back in harness again."

"I like seeing the girls, and being with other people than just my family."

"I got tired of coffee-clatching. I don't want to earn too much money . . . my husband's income tax, you know. . . . But what I make gives us the little extras, and it gets me away from the house. I love it."

These were typical comments.

The part-time workers in the second category have much the same motivation but do not feel free to take on part-time work on a regular basis. They told me variously:

"The money comes in mighty handy, especially at Christmas time and during the summer holidays when I usually work."

"It's exciting. A big sale can drive you crazy, but it's fun too. You sure learn a lot about human nature!"

"I can't be away every day on a regular basis, but my mother doesn't mind coming in to look after the kids for a week or two at a stretch. I give her a little something that she appreciates too, so we are both better off."

Still another group of women have themselves listed as available through some of the agencies that supply casual office help to employers. They are usually excellent workers who tend to be called to relieve or help out as substitutes in a few business concerns where the quality of their work is known. They are paid by the agency, which charges the employer a set fee and makes its profit through the difference between its charge and its payment to the woman employee.

Mavis works as often and as long as she wants to under this arrangement. She knows that she can make more money if she takes on a steady job, but she is not interested at this stage in her life. "This way," she told me, "I can pick and choose. I can work when I want to, and stay home when I have to, for instance, when one of the kids is sick or needs me for some other reason. My oldest daughter was married last month, and I just took my name off the list for two months before the wedding. I didn't have the pressure of going to work, and I didn't have to feel guilty that I was letting anyone down. Today I am back at work. I've been on this job for ten days and expect I'll be here for another two or three, as long as they need me to do the particular thing they called me for. This way I can book off for the summer, or if Jack decides that I should go on one of his business trips I'm free to go with him if I can get someone in to look after the younger children; I still don't like to leave them alone."

An older woman who retired from an office job about three years ago also uses this type of agency. "It's nice to have a little extra money for a trip without tying myself down to a job. Besides, I am too old to take on regular work. This way I can pick and choose my jobs and my days. No crawling out of bed and standing on a cold corner to catch a bus in January . . . if I don't want to. It's been a wonderful experience. You have no idea how much I have learned getting around the city as I do. And the nice people I've met. It's much better, you better believe it, than sitting in my little apartment looking at the four walls. And I'm useful. I must be pretty good or I wouldn't be called so often. That's nice to know at my age."

Part-time work has been a blessing to some of the young mothers who talked to me about it.

"We need the money right now, but I couldn't take on full-time work. The little bit I make working three or four hours a day makes all the difference between going into debt and keeping our heads above the water – just."

"No way could I handle three full-time jobs. Being a housekeeper and having the sort of social life my husband expects and raising two rambunctious kids are full-time jobs. But I have to get away from the house or I would go crazy. I worked for eight years before I got married. How could I suddenly transform my whole way of life? So I am listed with Office Overload and get just enough work to keep me from landing in a mental hospital! Don't take me seriously about the last remark! Although sometimes I felt you could take me seriously when the children were babies."

The part-time workers, their employers told me, are generally good. They also tend to be cheap. Few belong to pension plans or insurance plans to which the companies contribute. As they work by the hour or day, few accumulate seniority. They are on call, and their employers have little responsibility for them. The good ones have been around long enough to know the routine of the offices or stores in which they work, so that training is minimal.

"Yes, indeed," the manager of a large department in a retail store assured me, "these ladies are very valuable to us. A lot of them have been with us for years on a part-time basis; you know, they come in for a few hours a couple of days a week, or a couple of evenings a week when their husbands can look after the children. Others we call when we need them. Look at that lady over there, the one with the fancy hair-do. She worked in our department for ten years before and after she was married, and she comes in now only maybe for five or six weeks a year, for the big sales and for the Christmas rush. She's a good girl. She knows everyone around here, and how things are done. I ask for her whenever I am short of help."

Part-time work, then, fills a need both for the female worker and for the employer. The majority of women who work part time need the money. It seems unjust that in so many instances they have not been able to acquire salary increments, insurance and pension benefits. I was told by some of them that certain companies – which they refused to name because they did not want to jeopardize future employment – have an unstated but well-known policy never to keep part-time help to the point where the women become eligible for vacation pay. Other employers were cited as keeping part-time workers on minimum pay although their experience and the fact that they came back repeatedly to do the same kind of work for the companies might have warranted a rise in the rate of pay. When a woman complained, or even raised the question without complaining, she was labelled a troublemaker and her services were not used again.

One of the employers whom I questioned said candidly that in his case, anyway, his business was benefiting by using part-time women workers. They are generally glad to have the work, don't worry too much about the working conditions because they don't think of them as permanent, often don't even know what deductions are made from their pay cheques or pay envelopes. Best of all, they don't have to be kept on during slack times. A woman employer said that her shop could not be operated without part-time help. It wasn't economical to keep on five full-pay employees who "sat around drinking coffee" during most of the day when two full-time women were sufficient during the morning and late afternoon. Six would be used during the rush hours – in her business, during the noon hour and from about two to four in the after-noon. "So I have one woman and myself on full time (I put in two full days every day myself!) and hire four really good girls from 12.30 to 4.30. They like it, and it saves me money. They've worked here for years and know the customers, etc. Yes, they are eligible for unemploy-ment insurance – I've never fired one of them – and pay into the Canada Pension, but of course they can't build up much there because their actual pay is small and their working time limited."

I talked with one of the "girls," a middle-aged woman who had worked part time ever since her children had begun school; all but one were now away from home. "Part-time work is just right for me," she said. "The hours are perfect for my schedule and my husband's. Why should I waste my afternoons? Pension? No, I won't have one except from the government, but then I wouldn't have had one if I had stayed home all my life, would I? I wouldn't even have had the Canada Pension."

From Marguerite Bourgeoys, raising money for New France, to Mrs. Provenski trudging the hot streets with her farm produce, from Margaret Brown typing with four fingers to Maggie, at the same time fighting her way up and combating racism, from Colleen working at low-paid jobs because she can't afford to upgrade herself to Edith, who turned her small skills into a profitable enterprise, women in Canada have had a long history in business. They have come to it from every part of the country, from every ethnic group, from every age grouping. They have brought to it a variety of levels of education and a wide variety of experience. Most of them have received considerable satisfaction from their work, especially when it dealt with people and held some challenge. Not all of them have had the same kind of motivation; not all of them have thought of it in terms of careers, but most of them have needed the fruits of their labour desperately and were willing to work hard and with loyalty and devotion.

Most of them have been underpaid in terms of the jobs they do and of the pay their male colleagues receive. Few of them have made it to the top. For the most part they are wrapped in the cloak of invisibility, neither seen nor thought of when opportunities for promotion crop up in their companies. For the most part they are the shadowy invisible army of workers who keep business running, occasionally sergeants, rarely, very rarely, generals.

The young man at the bank who has taken my order for a gift certificate sits down at the nearest typewriter and slowly, hesitantly, pecks out the few words required to fill in the form: the name and address of the registered owner, the date, the amount of the certificate. He makes a mess of the first attempt, rips up the form and fills in a second one. When he brings it to me he has misspelled the name, although I had handed him a slip of paper with the name printed on it.

3

Preparing for a Business Career

"Sorry," he says. "As you can see, I have never learned to type."

Yes, I can see. I can also see that at the two other typewriters young women are quickly and efficiently filling in other forms for customers. I ask the young man, a pleasant chap, obviously not too long out of high school, whether he has had any specific training for the job he is doing.

"Oh, no," he answers, "but I have sure learned a lot since I've been here. Four months yesterday." Then he volunteers the information that he will be leaving soon for the downtown branch to get more experience and training.

A young woman working at one of the typewriters recognizes me and comes over to speak to me. Six years ago at the age of fourteen, an age at which she would already have left school in her native land, she had come from Italy without a word of English. In the intervening years she has finished high school, over her father's protests, she told me. In Italy she would have been engaged, or even married, before our legal school leaving age of sixteen. Her father had been so unpleasant about her going to school that she had left home and gone to live with her married sister and had attended a large composite high school with a strong vocational component.

"A wonderful place. They understood my problems and that English was difficult for me. The counsellor thought business English, shorthand and typing would be useful to me, and I followed her advice. Very good advice. In Grade 11 I also took a bit of accounting. Gee, Miss Shack, I never thought I would work in a BANK!" Her awe at the status she had attained in such a short time in Canada shone in her eyes and echoed in her voice. "My teachers gave me good references. One of them phoned the manager here and asked him if he had an opening. He didn't then, but he said he would keep me in mind. You know, I didn't believe him. I thought he was just being nice to me, but a couple of weeks later

I was called in for an interview and a test, and I got the job! And here I am." Her voice was full of exclamation marks.

Giuliana and the young man represent what is often the female and the male preparation for low-level jobs in business. The young man did not need typing and shorthand, although he did mention that he had had a course in accounting somewhere along the way. Giuliana is not too different (except for her immigrant status) from thousands of young women who equip themselves to make a living by taking business education programs at high school, and who then move directly into the labour force.

What is the business education program in high school and who goes into it? Does it do the job it is supposed to do? What opinion do teachers, students, employers have about it?

Dr. Geraldine Farmer, Associate Professor at the Faculty of Education of the University of Alberta and a former president of the Canadian Association of Business Education Teachers, speaking in 1970, saw as a major problem of high school business education "its isolation or detachment . . . from the core or centre of the educational system. Business education appears to be an appendage to that which is good, and it appears to be for those who find intellectual pursuits difficult or unattractive." High school teachers with whom I discussed this matter agreed wholeheartedly with Dr. Farmer's assessment of the situation, especially with the second part of her comment.

"We're lucky to get middle or average students. Most of those who come to us are the low students who have never been particularly successful at school."

"Above-average or average students aim for the university. The gates of heaven open if you go to university, or so they seem to think."

"We do our damnedest to give the kids the kinds of skills they can apply immediately after leaving school, and we provide a wide variety of courses, everything from key punching and filing to advanced office practice. It's just too bad that parents, teachers, and students don't realize that there is quality and challenge in business education . . . and that a very high percentage of general program students will be going into business and have to take courses later on, or be handicapped because they hadn't had the training."

"As a business education teacher I know how important intelligence is to success in the business world, especially for a woman. If it were up to parents and academic teachers we would always get the deadwood in business ed. We're just lucky that some of the girls are smarter than their

44

fathers, mothers, and teachers. They're anxious to get out into the working world; they want to be independent. So they enrol in business ed courses in high school. What a joy to teach them! Yes, I think there are more and more high calibre students coming into business ed."

"We get another kind of kid who is a good student, the girl or boy who wants typing, especially, but some of the other business options like communications that we also offer. These students don't think of themselves as taking business ed. They know they'll have to type notes and essays at college or university, or they have heard their friends talking about the interesting offerings in communications and human relations courses. They often take these courses as extras, or non-credit options."

"Even though I am a business ed teacher I wouldn't let my daughter take it. That's not because the program in our school is bad or anything, but because it cuts her off too early. I don't want her to get into a routine office job at seventeen or eighteen and stay there. I tell her that she'll have plenty of time to go into business education at a higher level, say at the local community college. I don't want her to specialize at her age. There's too much to learn and to do for her to spend her time in high school in subjects that are so oriented to drill and practice, like shorthand and typing."

Speaking again in 1974 Dr. Farmer expressed the belief that her earlier concern regarding the isolation and low prestige of business subjects is no longer as great as it had been. "Business education," she said, "seems to be assuming its proper and equal place with the traditional subjects. . . . The prestige hierarchy is being disturbed because we are swiftly moving into an era of student value-tagged courses; the era of the administrator, teacher or department of education value-tagged courses is disappearing. . . . Thus if students' interests and needs are permitted to govern, a given course could have as many values placed upon it as there are students."

And the students? How do they feel about the business education program they receive in high school? There seems to be about the same range of opinion as among their teachers. Some, like Giuliana, think the courses are excellent, a fine preparation for work. Others are not quite as enthusiastic but are nevertheless appreciative; still others are almost entirely negative.

Betty, twenty-one, works in the office of a large construction firm. There are about twenty other women in the office. "Yeah, I guess I learned a lot at high school. Anyway it was enough to get me my first job. The shorthand I have used a little; my typing was okay, but not really as good as it should have been. I was careful but too slow; I've improved my speed since. And I never saw the kind of equipment we use in our office. I guess the school can't afford to buy it because they still don't have it. I guess it didn't matter very much because I learned to use it when I had to."

Doreen found her business ed courses at high school dull and boring, and most of it, she said, useless. She's had a job doing filing, but her typing wasn't good enough for her to keep a general office job. "Maybe some day I'll go back and brush up on my typing, that is, if I don't get married. I'm not ashamed to admit that I want to get married and have a home and kids."

Students I talked with in a large composite high school with heavy enrolment in business programs complained that the courses were old-fashioned: this in spite of the fact that their school provides work-study experience and more than twenty options over a two- or three-year period of study. One student said to me, "It's too bad our teachers don't go out more often for work experience. I'm sure some of them have never worked in an office or anywhere in business, or if they have it's so long ago that they've forgotten what it's really like. Some of them still talk about the forty-four-hour week and taking home work to do!"

She was totally wrong about her teachers' experience. Almost without exception they were young people themselves, all of them with business experience – their board would not hire anyone without it – and planning to use an almost mandatory leave of absence for another stint in what the student called "the real world." When I mentioned the forty-four-hour week, one of them said, "Ye gods, you have to be careful about what you say to some of these kids. Yeah, I must be the one she's talking about. Sure, I was telling them how much better off their generation is . . . NO forty-four-hour week!"

Business education teachers agree with Dr. Farmer that the past few years have seen a marked improvement in high school business education programs, with a general upgrading of teachers' qualifications and a new emphasis on the use of modern methods in teaching. The new technical-vocational schools that have been built across the country are well-equipped. "It's impossible to teach the new technology unless you have the equipment of the new technology," more than one teacher said to me.

Girls still outnumber boys anywhere from two to one to ten to one in many business courses. Exceptions are typing and occasionally forms of accounting and computer science, where boys have enrolled in increasing numbers. Communications, human relations, and economics courses have also attracted boys. Said one counsellor, "Remember, before you condemn us for directing the girls into business education and the boys into other vocational courses, that there are far more opportunities outside of an office for boys. Take a tour of our big vocational high school and just notice how many programs are really oriented to boys' needs rather than girls'. Okay, you can tell me that we should be sending our girls into the 'boys' ' courses, but they don't want to go; and if they did they'd still have a tough time being placed in a job, whereas we can place as many as we turn out in business. Don't let your women's lib theories blind you to the realities of life."

I must say that I was frequently directed towards the realities of life, especially when I questioned the status quo. I am not exactly blinded to them, merely sad that girls who on aptitude tests rate low on mathematical and clerical skills and high on mechanical reasoning are shunted into business education and kept out of automotive shops. The stereotypes fade slowly, even in the minds of counsellors who should know better.

Over the years I have listened to many complaints about the quality of students our high schools turn out into the business world. Occasionally I have almost, but not quite, joined the ranks of the complainers. As for example when I received a form letter in reply to a request for materials from an eastern company. The opening sentence read: "We are sorry to dissapoint you in that we cannot accomodate your order."

If I had sent the letter back to the signer, whose illegibly scrawled signature was mimeographed at the bottom of it, and had drawn attention to the dreadful "business English" and the misspellings, he would probably have remarked, as I have heard other businessmen remark, that he is too busy to check all the form letters that go out over his name. It's his "girl's" business to make sure that they are properly set up, typed, spelled. Besides, he was never a good speller himself, and that's why he has a secretary, to look after these things for him. Why weren't the schools doing a better job? What kind of training do the girls get, anyway?

The answer to that question is complex, because young women are prepared for their jobs in business in many different ways, the high school business education program being only one of them. Even within the high school program there are many possibilities. In Manitoba, which seems in many respects to be reasonably typical, in 1974 the high school business education program was divided into three main categories: Secretarial, Accounting, Marketing. Girls were in the first of the three in overwhelming numbers, with generally more boys in the other two. In the total business education program there were far more young women than young men. Then within each of the major categories there was a variety of options, depending on the size, the resources, and the orientation of the school offering them. As the business education teachers had pointed out, the range of ability and ambition of students entering business education is broad, and a satisfactory program must be prepared to offer many choices. Only in that way is it possible to meet not only the needs of business but also the needs of people who are to work in business, to lay the groundwork for employment in jobs of widely varying complexity, difficulty, responsibility.

High school business education programs must have considerable value. In a survey conducted by the Winnipeg Chamber of Commerce in 1974, 71 per cent of members responding indicated that they would rather hire a young person who had graduated from a high school business education program than one who had had a general education. Business education teachers in cities as widely separated and different as Victoria, Saskatoon, Winnipeg, Montreal told me that they had no trouble placing their graduates if the students had had even moderate success in the business education programs. "Mind you, not always in particularly good jobs, or jobs with a future, but then," said a teacher in Montreal, "it is up to them after that, isn't it? We do our best for them; we get them started, and then it is up to them to better themselves or to settle into a rut."

"Remember," said a friend of mine who has taught business education for many years, indeed, in the days when it was called "Commercial," "remember that business education covers a wide range of subjects and a wide range of ability among students. A lot of the kids we are carrying through business courses nowadays would never have made it as far as high school in the so-called good old days. We are dipping pretty deep into the population pool to meet the demands of business and government. When you and I were growing up the girls who are now going into offices would have gone into domestic service or, if they were lucky, into the factories."

My friend is, of course, right. Looking back to the distribution of female labour even as late as 1921 and 1931 it is clear that a mighty shift has taken place. The "servant" has disappeared, and many so-called personal service jobs require as long and as arduous training as the average office worker or store clerk gets, often longer and more arduous training.

Moreover, when I graduated from high school there were really only three options open to female graduates who had to earn a living: nursing, teaching, business. Canadian business, smaller and less complex in scope in those years, had a large number of intelligent, eager, compliant women from which to choose. These intelligent, eager, if not nearly as compliant women now have a wider choice of career, not only in the trades and professions but also within business itself. Many of the options open to them are intrinsically more interesting and often pay better than the routine office jobs that women once accepted without question as their due – or their fate. Business is not alone in having lost its primacy of appeal. Teaching and nursing have also suffered from the competition.

As openings for women in business have expanded, a broader range of the total female population has been recruited. As my friend pointed out, a variety of jobs exists to meet the needs of the highly qualified and capable and of the less qualified and less capable. School counsellors, personnel officers, and employers should be screening and selecting not on the basis of age or sex but on the basis of ability to handle the job and to be challenged by it at both ends of the scale of responsibility.

The Winnipeg Chamber of Commerce in a brief submitted to a special Task Force on Business Education (December 1974) shared with Dr. Farmer and other educational leaders the opinion that it is unwise to separate business education students from the general stream. "The separation of programs at the student level can lead to elitist thinking on one hand and Mickey Mouse labels on the other," the Chamber of Commerce brief states, and Dr. Farmer quotes an Alberta high school principal as saying, "I have one large high school having all kinds of students and I attempt to avoid identifying these students as belonging to the technical department, business department, or the academic department. This separation aspect is played down at all times."

So while the technical-vocational high schools in both large and small centres have large technical and vocational components, they have also almost always kept their strong academic bent. Particularly in smaller population centres the technical-vocational school is less that than a composite secondary school, serving the total spectrum of high school students in a community.

Sylvia Lepine is president and principal-administrator of the Robertson Secretarial School, a private business school in Saskatoon. I asked her to comment on the calibre of girls taking business education, on their aspirations, and on secretarial training generally from her point of view as the principal of a private business school.

"We have a high calibre of girls and women," she said. "All have at least high school graduation. The best students are those who have been out of high school for a year or two. We get university students and university graduates from all the faculties, former teachers and nurses and those who have worked for anywhere up to ten or more years as well as women returning to the work force after their families are grown.

"As I see them, eighteen-to-twenty-year-olds, as always, feel that they will be married in a couple of years and that, despite evidence to the contrary all around them, all their problems will be solved or they will have no problems once they are married. Anyway they won't have to work. Many who do plan to work usually do so to help a husband get his education or to get him established in a career without any thought of what happens if things don't work out. This is part of a generally unrealistic attitude," Mrs. Lepine added.

She, like so many others in the field of business education, was concerned about the attitude of many people towards business and business training particularly. "Secretarial training, and business training generally, have been so downgraded by the academics that secretaries have never enjoyed the status they deserved. So many of our good students come to us bitter and disillusioned; the comments most usually made are, 'We are never told anything good about the business world,' or 'We were never given any information at all.' They are surprised and delighted with the challenge and opportunities and become annoyed when friends and former teachers infer that they are taking a 'nothing' course. A proper, a good secretarial course is very demanding and sets high standards of performance. Qualified, highly skilled secretaries are always in short supply. Because of the importance of communication in this world I predict that the status of secretaries will rise sharply. Employers are already aware of the situation, and there is a sharp distinction between the position of 'secretary' (executive, private, confidential) and the steno-clerk-typist or other junior-type office clerk. Because employers are changing their attitudes, and making the distinctions, you will find that women will become more concerned about qualifications."

Almost to a women the people who answered my own questionnaire agreed with Mrs. Lepine that educational qualifications were important, without limiting themselves to secretarial studies. Twenty-one of ninety respondents had taken their business education at high school and had no further formal business education; they had learned specific skills on the job. Many more had had short courses or additional training at proprietary schools like Mrs. Lepine's. Some had had all their pre-job training at a community college or technical-vocational institute. Most of them believed that the minimum training given in the high schools, at least in their day, was not sufficient, particularly for women who planned on business as a career, or who wanted to rise beyond the lowest levels of the business world. To make real progress, women, they said, should have a sound business education and specialized business training well beyond high school.

It is therefore not strange that the community colleges, CEGEPs, and technical institutes across the country have developed large and flourishing business education sections. These institutions were created (or expanded) with the help of federal funds to meet the needs of post-secondary students who were looking for alternatives to the universities, generally with vocational colour, and though they have developed somewhat differently in the different regions of Canada, by and large they are trying to live up to their principal objective.

Some, like Dawson College in Montreal, are large complex institutions. (Dawson is spread through six campuses, Seneca in Toronto over five.) Others are like Keewatin in northern Manitoba, which has a small enrolment and serves the specific needs of its unique community. Most offer business education courses similar to those being given to school-aged students in the high schools; generally these are packaged into one-year programs (ten months, or anywhere from forty to fifty-two weeks), and therefore have over the years qualified for funding under Canada Manpower provisions. In addition, all those I investigated have short programs in which adults who have had previous business training or experience can come back to brush up their skills; and the larger colleges or institutions offer two-, three-, and, in a few cases, four-year programs leading to diplomas in various aspects of business practice, and in business management and business administration. Several of the colleges have working agreements with universities in the same communities whereby credits for equivalent work can be transferred from one institution to another, so that courses taken at the colleges can "count" towards a degree in commerce or business administration, and university courses where they parallel college courses may be credited towards standing at the college level.

In the secretarial one-year program, the enrolment in most of the colleges or technical-vocational institutes is almost totally female, 90 per cent or more in some of them. There are, however, some options within the one-year program, or the program bears a different title, in order to accommodate different courses. Some women are in clerk-typist programs (of six to ten months' duration), some in stenography (ten months), some in accountancy (ten months), a few in marketing or commercial and industrial sales.

I talked with women students at several colleges. One of them was Lucy, at Keewatin College in The Pas, Manitoba. She had come up to business education by way of the Basic Training for Skills Development program, having left school in her native Nova Scotia at the end of Grade 5. Actually, if she wanted to take her training in her home town she had little choice; she could choose either beauty culture or stenography, so she was in the latter. She is an intelligent young woman by anyone's standards, divorced, with two children to support. In Nova Scotia she had worked as a waitress at the age of fourteen in order to help raise her younger brothers and sisters. She married young, and she and her husband moved to northern Manitoba to look for work. She found it; he didn't, and eventually, she said, "he just drifted off, and after a while I divorced him. No, I don't know where he is, and I don't care. I have learned to be independent." Lucy was promised a job in one of the northern mining towns as soon as she finished her course. She is being funded under Canada Manpower.

Joan is reasonably typical of another group of students in the one-year (forty-week, ten-month) program at the post-secondary level. She is taking a clerical-bookkeeping course at a community college in a middle-sized city. She is a pleasant-looking person, but I would not be able to describe her now, several months after I met her, had I not made a note of her appearance. She is blondish, was dressed like a great many other eighteen-year-olds whom I had seen; she used almost no make-up. I did notice that her nails had been bitten to the quick, and though she spoke with confidence and showed considerable poise – she, like the other students I spoke to at the colleges, had volunteered for the interview – she waited for the others to speak before she ventured an opinion. She had been born and had gone to school in a small town about a hundred miles from the city where she was now living with an older sister, in an apartment "too far from the college for comfort. It takes me nearly three-quarters of an hour to get here in the morning on the bus and longer to get home at night because I have to fight the traffic."

When Joan finished high school, in an academic program, she did not have any strong feelings about what she wanted to do. She had not been a particularly good student at school.

"I didn't know where to start," she told me. "But my parents thought I should get some training. My sister took me somewhere and I wrote a test that showed that I had a little more aptitude for clerical work than for anything else. The man that gave me the test, a friend of my brother-in-law, said I didn't show any strong preferences but that I'd probably do all right in office work. So I went down and enrolled at the college. One of my girl friends had started there a few months before, and she helped me find my way around. The course is for ten months, and all together with books and fees and everything it'll cost me about two hundred dollars. My family is paying my sister for my room and board; I have enough saved up from birthday money and gifts and a little baby-sitting for pocket money and my books. No, I didn't apply for a loan. My family doesn't believe in borrowing money. My father sends me a bit every month. I am managing nicely. No, I couldn't manage if my mother and dad weren't right behind me; and my sister and her husband have been pretty good to me too. I try not to be a nuisance. I know it can't be much fun for them to have to worry about me. A boy friend? No, not really. No, I haven't met anyone at the college. You don't get to see anyone much outside your own class, and there sure aren't any boys in the course I'm taking."

Did she like the course? "It's okay. I really enjoy the accounting. It's funny. I never cared much for math at school, but this I like."

Joan has never worked and would like to have the experience of "having a boss." She would like to work in a small office, not in a large pool, "I guess because I come from a small town. I get kind of scared of big places. I was sure scared of this place when I first came. I kept on getting lost. If I hadn't had a friend I think I would have quit after a week."

Joan finds the workload heavy. There is never enough time in class to finish assignments – maybe, she thinks, because she is kind of a slow worker and a slow reader. So she stays sometimes and works in the evening, if someone else is staying who lives in the same direction. She doesn't like the long ride home, and the dark walk from the bus stop to the apartment, especially on winter nights. What is she taking? Let's see: Accounting, Business Machines, Office Procedures, Business Mathematics, Basic Typewriting, Business Communications. She could have a course, without credit, in physical education, but she's kind of shy about getting out in the gym. She's afraid she'd look silly. She's sure the kids who take phys ed are athletic types, and with her figure – well. Anyway, she needs the time to work on her other subjects, and there's no credit for the phys ed.

Donna represents another segment of the many women enrolled in the one-year program in business education at the colleges or institutes. She has been married for three or four years, worked for a store "doing books" – "just picked it up when the girl that had the job before showed me how." Her husband wanted to go back to school. It was through his investigations of possibilities for getting help that she found out about Canada Manpower. The Manpower people decided that she had enough skills, however, and wouldn't sponsor her, so she is on her own. Her husband was accepted into a program in business administration, got the money, she isn't quite sure how, from two or three different sources, one of them being a student loan. She is working part time, some evenings and every Saturday. That doesn't give her much time to study, and the program she is in, Counselling and Industrial Sales, a ten-month program, is heavy, but she feels stimulated by it. She is taking courses called Consumer Behavior, Personnel, Selling and Advertising, Report Writing.

Yes, her husband is very co-operative. He pitches in and helps, that is, when he has the time. He is also working very hard, and finds his studies difficult. She's looked at his books and thinks she could handle most of them, though they are hard to read. She won't need to take business admin. Not after she's been through the course with David. They both complain that most of the textbooks are American, though some have been revised to suit the Canadian situation. At least the teachers are Canadian and can help interpret the Canadian scene.

Marta looks as tough as nails and talks a blue streak, as her friend Theresa told her more than once during the course of our conversation. Marta began our interview with the remark that she loathed working with women: "With men, you come in singing." Her nails were long and bright red. "My typing teacher thinks I should file them down, but no way. I showed her I could type better with my finger tips than all them mousy gals with their chewed-off nails. I know, I know, don't bother me. I shouldn'ta said *them gals*. Miss What's-her-name's got me brainwashed. . . . So, *those* gals. Okay? I'm learning."

Marta got no advice from anyone; she had to find out the hard way, but finally when she'd been on unemployment insurance for a while she convinced "them idiots at Manpower" to get her into a program. "I'm gonna pull myself up in the world. Nobody's going to look after little old Marta but me." She'd worked as a nurse's aide after a six-week course; then she'd been a waitress in hotels and beverage rooms. "Boy, oh boy, you shoulda seen me in my outfit."

But she got tired of the work and everything that went with it. There was no future in it, and she felt she was too smart for it. The hours were bad, the work was hard. So she got herself a job in a general insurance office. "I don't know how," she said, "because I didn't have any of the qualifications. I guess it was hard to get help, and I was a little older than most of the girls who were looking for work."

Marta paused for a moment. "As a matter of fact," she said, "I really couldn't hold the job, 'cause I didn't know enough. I was fired. That's when I decided I'd have to go back to school. So here I am. Ten years out of school, and back at the books again. You think I'm loud. Lady, if you only knew it I was never more scared in my life."

Theresa told me that Marta didn't have to be scared. She was a leader in the class and a fast learner. Two of her teachers corroborated Theresa's opinion both in Marta's presence and afterwards over a cup of tea. "She's loud, all right, but there's a lot of common sense there, and not an ounce of laziness in her make-up. She needs confidence, and we are trying to give it to her. She's in a Communications program which tries to heighten awareness. It's been interesting to see what it has done for Marta."

"What about this business of loathing to work for women?" I asked Marta.

"Well," she said, "women, you know women. They're *fussy*. Nothing's ever right for them. They're jealous if the men in the place even look at you. Nah, I don't like working for women."

"Have you ever worked for a woman?" I asked.

"Yeah, I guess I could say I have. When I was a nurse's aide. And the head girl in the office that I got fired from. Mind you, if you gotta know, she wasn't all that bad. I kinda liked her. The fella who told me I was fired said she'd tried to have me kept on a while longer. But I don't know. It ain't . . . I mean it isn't . . . like working for a man. A man, I don't know, it makes me feel like I'm working for a real boss."

"What about your teachers? Do you prefer men or women teachers?"

"Gee, I never thought about it. It don't, I mean, it *doesn't* — ee-ee, you see I'm learning! — it doesn't matter. That's different. They're teachers."

The teachers informed me that in the ten-month or forty-week business education programs most of the women were relatively young, many of them straight out of high school, although there was a healthy sprinkling of people like Marta and Donna and many who, like the students in the sixteen-week program, were the heads of families or married women returning to work after a long absence. In clerical and stenographic programs, as in the high schools, the enrolment is overwhelmingly female.

Diane Fried, chairman of the section on secretarial studies at Seneca College, made the observation that when girls finish Grade 12 the "business and commercial types feel that there is only one way to go — secretarial. For some of them the secretarial course is really a postponement of going to work. They think they'll be better off if they specialize, as of course they may well be." A survey of first-semester students in the one-year (ten-month) secretarial course a couple of years ago showed that the majority came from homes with an income range of twelve to twenty thousand dollars a year, and they rather unrealistically expected to earn within the same range.

The most common reason given for coming to Seneca was that the young women did not want to go to work right away. The most important influence in making the decision where to go was their parents', followed fairly closely by that of their friends. They went hoping that as a result they would earn higher salaries, gain a greater development of their technical skills.

A similar survey in the second semester of their program proved that if they had learned nothing else, they had learned to adjust their expectations of future earnings. They were far more realistic.

Students agreed with teachers that often they were directed into secretarial programs simply because there seemed no other place to go. The feeling was general; it was conveyed to me at Dawson and at Red River and by some graduates of Camosun and of the Prairie Institutes of Applied Arts and Technology as well as at Keewatin. Female foreign students, particularly, were sometimes shunted into secretarial programs when it was obvious that they were bright and capable.

"Teaching or office work or nursing," said one young woman from Hong Kong. "I got stuck in a secretarial course and I was totally lost because though I had school English I was not fluent enough to cope with business English. Imagine me struggling with shorthand! The syllables didn't sound the same to me as they did to my instructor. After a few months I was able to laugh about it, but I spent a lot of time crying about it before I could laugh." She's doing fine right now, thank you, but not because of her secretarial course. She operates a novelty shop in an "arty" section of a West Coast city and has brought out two sisters to join her. "When their English is good enough one is going to take accounting and the other one – she's what you call a little dynamo – something in sales and advertising. Then we'll have a chain of stores. You'll see."

Then there were students in the two- and three-year programs in various aspects of business education. For the two-year course most of the colleges expect a minimum of Grade 12 standing, but many open their doors to mature students who are selected on the basis of past experience, an entrance examination, and/or a personal interview. More and more of the college departments now believe that a mature person should have the opportunity to try a program and to fail out or drop out of it or change its direction if she cannot handle her original ambitious plans. Thus the purely academic requirements are often by-passed in favour of other qualifications.

As an example, Seneca College in Toronto offers a two-year diploma program to enable people to qualify as executive (business) secretaries. The brochure claims that "emphasis is placed on the role of the secretary in human and public relations; preparation of agendas, minutes and reports; planning of itineraries, travel arrangements and conferences; office procedures and practices necessary to assist an executive." Most of the first year of the program provides the basic training in typing, short-hand, and secretarial duties that are required "in all fields." The second year provides opportunities to specialize. Algonquin College in Ottawa offers much the same kind of program in its two-year secretarial course. Both Seneca and Algonquin offer as electives French as a second language. In Ottawa about 40 per cent of the students in the secretarial course are taking it. In addition to the basics that appear in all secretarial (or stenographic-clerical) programs in the second year there is an opportunity for specializing: data processing, medical, legal, library, and in Ottawa a course on the government of Canada, since by far the largest number of graduates of the secretarial programs enter government service at one level or another. In most of the secretarial programs a course in English, whether business English or report writing or the structure of English, is mandatory.

As in the one-year programs, most of the women students in the longer programs are enrolled in the secretarial courses. There is, however, a growing interest in programs named variously Business Administration, Management Training, Advanced Marketing and Sales, Computer Analysis and Programming. A growing interest, but slow progress. In some colleges I was told that the number of women in the two-year business administration program, leading to a diploma, had doubled in two years. I was quite excited until I heard that there were now six women enrolled in the program where there had been three two years ago. Another administrator informed me that their female enrolment in a management course had increased by 200 per cent as a result of greater awareness on the part of companies. His department now had nine women as compared with eighty men. "Crackerjacks, all of them," he said with admiration.

Were they token women as far as their employers were concerned? I asked.

"Well, maybe they started out that way, because a lot of the big outfits like to be trendy, and the right thing now is to have a woman they can show off at the management level. But every one of these women is first class. Some of them were sent by their companies, but more than half of them are here on their own. Whoever gets them when they leave us is going to be lucky. They know how to throw themselves wholeheartedly into anything they are doing."

Not all the department heads in business admin courses were as enthusiastic about their female students. Said one man, "They tend to drop out sooner than the men. A man is usually in the program because he knows what he wants to do. He complains more if he isn't getting what he wants, and I suppose he has more influence over what is happening to him. The women aren't taken quite as seriously." He thought for a moment and added, "I guess that's why more of them drop out. They take a lot of kidding, too, especially the first year, until they have shown how good they are. The funny thing is that after a while none of us really remember that they are women. Do you understand what I mean? It isn't that after class, or in class, we can't appreciate that they look nice, smell good, and are feminine, but in the heat of discussion, in seminars and workshops, they are part of the total class. Sex, gender . . . that's forgotten."

Arlene Enns, who was in the second year of a business administration program when we talked together, had come to the same conclusion, from the other side of the table. In her class, too, more women than men dropped out at the end of the first year. "I think they just got tired of going to school," she said. "I had something of the same feeling myself. Besides, let's face it. Some of the drop-outs were women who didn't have to work. They thought when they started out that they wanted to be businesswomen, to be on the same footing as their husbands, but it meant too much work. Frustrated because they had so little influence? Perhaps. I know in my first year I got very tired of being condescended to. I knew that I was just as smart as most of the men in the class; there were a couple who were smarter, but not because they were men. As a matter of fact, I also had a lot more business experience than most of them. Some of them had come cold from high school. They'd never earned a dollar in their lives on a long-term basis. I had. I've done a lot of things – worked in offices, in stores, baby-sitting when I was a kid, shovelling snow – yeah, shovelling snow – and delivering newspapers."

Why was she in a business administration course? "Because I want to be my own person, have something responsible to do, not always be doing something for someone else. I was ready to quit one of my jobs when my boss – he really wasn't my boss: I just did some of his steno-graphic work for him – anyway, I was ready to quit when he asked me to buy his wife's birthday present and address invitations for a cocktail party he and his wife were giving. Well, I didn't quit until I had some-thing better to go to, because I have to work for my living. Now I am thinking about a long-term career. I may get married; I may not. Either way I am a businesswoman."

Arlene was paying her own way, every bit of it, by working part time as a cosmetics saleswoman in a department store. She's good. It's a field she is interested in, and she hopes she will be able to specialize in that aspect of marketing: advertising, personnel, consumer behaviour, and so on. She makes enough in wages and commission so that she can just manage the two-year program without using up all her savings. "Not that I should worry about that. At the rate of inflation we are into now my money is fading away anyway. I might as well spend it on something that will help me earn more."

I had mentioned to her the comment of the department head who said that after a while the class and the teachers forgot that the female students were women and thought of them simply as fellow members in the club.

"Right on," she said. "I never had a guy as a *friend* before in my life." She emphasized the word "friend." "I'm *friends* with some of the guys in the class. I really enjoy being treated as a person. During the first year I took some teasing about women's lib, and I learned to laugh and kid right back instead of getting mad. Now the boys accept me for what I can do and what I am and don't worry about bra burning or other silliness. They respect my work, too, and we share ideas and work on projects together. It's just great."

Arlene does not have much time to study, and like some of the one-year students she finds the program heavy because she is working part time. "No holidays for me until I get my diploma. Then I'm going to splurge before going to work full time again. Anyway I think I'll splurge. It'll be just my luck to have a job offered to me that I have to take right away!"

Arlene made an important point. During the entire length of her program she has not had one woman teacher. She misses having women teachers. "They treat their female students differently from most men teachers – not all men teachers, but an awful lot of them. Men teachers tend to treat you as a pretty girl, not as a serious student in what they, subconsciously maybe, consider to be a man's field. One of my men teachers commented during the course of a conversation – I don't think he meant to be insulting, he just said it because that's what he thought – that a girl just comes here to get a guy. I was mad, but there was no use arguing with him. Men making snide remarks do it because they are uncomfortable with women. Sometimes they make remarks they don't even mean just to show that they are masculine, whatever that is."

At Humber College in Toronto a women's club was formed specifically to deal with women's problems and to give mutual support. One of the major problems was that mentioned by Arlene and by the department head of one of the business ed sections, the failure to take women students seriously. A former teacher at Humber, a woman now with a provincial Women's Bureau, noted the subtle discrimination being exercised against the female students by some male teachers. "It's an attitude. It's in the air. It's very subtle. Many male teachers have come to the colleges straight from business. They think, and say, that they know 'where it's at' – now, not some time in an ideal future – and they guide girls into the world 'as it is.' "

Another problem this woman saw among female students was the failure to develop potential because of generally low expectations, low on the part of families, on the part of the students themselves, on the part of teachers, and above all, on the part of employers. The employers do not want women who are too smart, unless, of course, they hide their intelligence sufficiently to preserve the bosses' self-esteem. "If we don't expect much from women, we won't get much."

"On the other hand," said a former colleague of hers, "there *is* the problem that the male teachers tend to use cynically. Suppose girls' expectations are raised on the basis of what they are capable of doing, and what they should be doing, and then those expectations are not met, as very often they are not? Teachers, counsellors, above all the women themselves, must face up to the difference between the wish and what actually is. Counsellors must be realistic about what the girls will meet when they go out into the cold, cruel world. How do we strike a reasonable balance between pushing our women students into unrealistic expectations, and squashing their potential for development by expecting too little for them?"

Both women supplied part of the answer. "Show them what is possible. Don't close doors in their faces before they have tried to open them. Don't automatically steer them to what is easiest. Let them know that they will have problems if they aim for what is not the traditionally female job. Give them the kind of help and support they need to work out solutions for the problems. Give them assistance in assessing their own ability and their personal goals. Then introduce them to many kinds of experiences so that they can make their choices intelligently, based on knowledge, awareness, and self-analysis. The so-called 'realities' are not immutable. We know plenty of women who have changed those realities because they were determined to change them."

Undoubtedly this is excellent advice in dealing with people like Lucy, of Keewatin College, who had drive and self-respect and courage; but what about the girls who drifted or were directed into business education because they had failed to qualify for other, more academically based programs? All their lives they had been failures, or at best had trailed behind the more gifted, more energetic, better socially and economically endowed students in their classes. They had seldom made conscious choices, their most positive response to suggestions often being a shrug of the shoulders or "I guess so."

Almost every teacher I spoke with expressed concern about these girls. They skipped classes; their assignments were rarely handed in on time; they seemed almost totally apathetic. Counsellors seemed to have little success in reaching them. Yet they were often girls of average or better than average intelligence, a fact they found difficult to accept. "How come you think I'm so smart," one young woman asked me, "when I get such bad marks?" And another told her frustrated counsellor, "Look. I'm sick and tired of being told that I can do this or that when I know that I can't, and what's the use anyway?"

These girls were in business education because the educational sorting system had sifted them out to what they considered the bottom of the barrel. They had no real interest in business and were going through the motions, either because their parents insisted that they remain at school, or because school supplied them with some kind of security and a circle of acquaintances. At least they knew what to expect there. The working world was more threatening.

Some members of this group are the truly underprivileged girls, those whose homes and total environment had failed to provide either the background for success or the stimulus that would help them, like Lucy, work their way out. They are girls from the core areas of large cities, girls from remote rural areas, girls drifting into the cities with families uprooted from the reservations. They are sometimes girls who through no fault of their own had inadequate schooling and inadequate preparation for the schooling they did get.

What to do for them? Obviously we must begin in a different way and use different approaches. "Don't condescend to these girls," a wise teacher advised. "And don't sound pitying or do-gooder, for heaven's sake. You'll turn them off before you start."

A social worker with years of experience in working with teen-aged girls and boys said, "We talk about teaching the life skills. These kids need to learn the fundamentals of how to walk and how to talk to people. They have to know how to dress and when to wear what, and how to use the little bit of money they have to the best advantage. They need building up of their confidence in themselves, and that's the way to do it, to make them feel that they are not gauche, awkward, out of place, and dumb. It's amazing how quickly their arrogance or their apathy – sometimes both – disappear when they get a little self-respect."

"I agree," said a teacher-counsellor. "Especially when you talk about money. I think one of the first things we have to do for kids like that is to have them feel the pleasure of earning money by doing an honest job. I push work-study programs: part time at school, part time at work, and being paid for the work. I should add that the work has to be carefully chosen and supervised so that it doesn't prove to be another failure, another kick in the ribs. By the way, why are there so many upgrading programs for men and so few for women?"

From Edmonton the owner and operator of a private school for receptionists agreed with the social worker about what constitutes life skills: knowing what to say and how to say it ranks high. Having confidence in one's appearance so that one can forget about it is also important.

A teacher of Communications told me that she was far more concerned with the ability of students to talk with one another and with their teachers and eventually their employers or customers than with the esoteric program laid out in the calendar under the heading of Communications; and at Algonquin College a young teacher outlined for me the program she was interested in devising that would help girls acquire the poise and self-confidence she believed they needed if they were to fit themselves for employment in any field.

Surely we have a responsibility to help these girls, not only for their sake, but also for the sake of society as a whole. Opportunities for success should be open to the total spectrum of women, not merely to those who already have built-in motivation and drive. As a teacher, and as a person who believes that education should provide a ladder for upward mobility, I am convinced that our high schools and our community colleges, our governmental provisions for upgrading and training should be paying particular heed to those women who need them most. Employees and employers would benefit. The knowledgeable, interested worker is happy and produces work of high quality; she is less likely to absent herself from the job and contributes to the healthy atmosphere of her place of employment. The apathetic, indifferent young woman like Doreen (page 46) is not much of an asset to any business firm; she is a victim of her own inadequacy, and perhaps of her background and training. Why should she find her business courses dull and boring and useless, when thousands of young women have found them interesting and exciting and a fine preparation for future employment?

At the other end of the spectrum there is a scattering of women in university courses that lead to a business degree, and an increasing number are working towards degrees in chartered accountancy – a long hard experience- and theory-based course – in commerce, marketing, business administration. Sometimes the value of the degree was questioned. "A good course in business admin or business practice or what have you at a community college is worth more than the university degree in practical terms," wrote one woman who had both.

"The degree is nice to have and looks good on a letterhead if you ever make one, but give me a woman who is intelligent and works hard and I'll train her on the job," another one said to me. Some of the women with a university background who wrote to me or whom I interviewed were not engaged in work bearing much relationship to their original studies; most, however, believed that their university studies were relevant to their employment.

"My degree gave me confidence," an Alberta real estate agent wrote. "I wasn't going to be put down by some ignoramus who spoke atrocious English. Maybe I was being snobbish, but I could always say to myself,

'Never mind. You know more than he does.' I said it to myself, and so I was able to keep my mouth shut and not say to him some of the undiplomatic things I might have. Then I did take psych and sociology. Both have been useful to me in the selling game." Two of my correspondents, one a professional engineer and one in a field where she would have benefited from being an engineer, pointed out that many engineers were in business and that architecture and engineering were logical jumping-off points for business. As is almost anything.

Statistics for 1970, however, are rather discouraging to women in the "women's jobs" like secretarial and stenographic work, or sales clerking.[1] They gain very little (at least in dollars and cents earned) by obtaining a university degree. In fact, many of them are at a disadvantage because they entered the labour force later, lost the earnings and pension benefits they might have accumulated during the years they spent in secondary and post-secondary schools and colleges. For instance, a female secretary between forty-five and fifty-four years old with Grade 8 standing or less would in 1970 have earned, on the average, $5,187. If she had devoted another ten or twelve years to attaining a master's degree or a doctorate, she might have reached the magnificent salary of $6,294. A male colleague doing the same kind of work at the same age with Grade 8 standing or less would have earned $8,019, and with a master's degree or doctorate he would have more than doubled his salary to $16,838. That is, through increased earnings a man rapidly recoups the cost of advanced education; a woman in the same position never regains in monetary terms what her education had cost her through lost salary, tuition, and maintenance costs. The situation is even more glaringly revealed in the area of sales. A woman sales clerk with Grade 8 standing or less at the age of fifty earned $3,431 as compared with a male clerk in the same classification who earned $6,256. The same woman if she had had a bachelor's degree would have been earning $3,922 to the man's $8,071.

As is not uncommon, the older woman is disadvantaged, though less disadvantaged because of her age than because of her sex. The young thing of twenty-five or thirty with her master's degree or her doctorate was already making substantially more than her fifty-year-old colleague: $7,715 to the older woman's $6,294. A young man in the same job would have averaged $13,584, about the same as his middle-aged friend's $13,260. In sales, the thirty-year-old with Grade 8 or less would have been earning a mere $3,230, compared with her male equivalent's $5,970 and her fifty-year-old female friend's $3,431. Experience is apparently of little value to employers of sales clerks, and education not much more.

The moral does not need underlining: Women with more than minimum educational qualifications should not allow themselves to be stalled in dead-end jobs.

Zelda Roodman, co-author with her husband of two books on management, is program manager for organizing courses for senior management at Algonquin College in Ottawa. She is impatient with women themselves and with government and with business and with senior management in business for not doing enough to get women involved in programs like hers. She has worked for a number of years to devise ways and means of getting women into management positions, senior management, as officers of their companies. She has set up Special Officers' Courses, and Advanced and Career Courses for Secretaries by request, and especially for women. In most of the programs offered by Algonquin – as in other college and university and continuing education programs – most of those attending are men. Part of the fault undoubtedly lies with the women, according to Dr. Roodman. They have not done their share in upgrading themselves. University women take Arts degrees that train them for nothing; at home they have been thoroughly indoctrinated to accept, indeed enjoy, passive roles. Of course there is male chauvinism, and male attitudes will also have to be changed. Dr. Roodman believes that legislation can change actions if not attitudes, and that as actions change, attitudinal change will also take place. Legislation is therefore imperative. Pressure must be put on industry that it will feel and will have to respond to; again, only legislation can exert that kind of pressure. Right now industry is not making any great effort to send its women to take management courses. And so the upgrading process is being neglected on three levels: by the women themselves, by business and industry, and by governments because their sanctions are not powerful enough to bring about equality of opportunity.

An encouraging note comes from universities and colleges that have recently set up credit courses in Women's Studies. Brochures advertising these courses list "Women in Management," "The Woman Administrator," "The Woman Executive," and "How to Live with Success."

Again and again I heard from women in positions of authority in education and in government: Women must help women. We have a responsibility to search out and encourage and fight for those women who have the ability to hold top-level jobs and are being kept from them because they are invisible in terms of promotion. Dr. Roodman cited the

65

case of Mary R., who came to take a two-week course in the Management Development program. During that time there was much talk about job enrichment and job upgrading and becoming part of the management team. Two months after the course was over Mary called to say that she was getting nowhere. Her boss had taken on an administrative trainee with no experience, a young man, who would inevitably block the girl's advancement. Dr. Roodman called Mary's boss, and on the basis of having known her ability through the course she had taken, persuaded him to give Mary more responsibility. She is now an administrative officer in her department. Mary was not being deliberately shoved aside; she was simply being overlooked, the invisible woman.

The Canadian government has a plan under which retired executives and administrators are sent to developing countries to help educators and business people in a direct and practical way by sharing their proven expertise. I suggest that the government or, if the government is slow and unwilling, women's organizations set up a similar process to help women who would like to go into business on a small scale but who have had no experience and do not know whom to ask or what to do, what first steps to take in becoming self-employed. An appreciable number of working women who answered my questionnaire indicated an interest in being self-employed but had no idea of what they might do, or how they would go about doing it. Women Executives Unlimited might be a source of ideas, a forum for discussion, as well as a pool from which individuals might be assigned to advise and assist on a one-to-one basis.

I am suggesting here a type of volunteerism that uses and recognizes talent and skill, an example of how women can help women directly, personally, and with gifts that no one else can bestow.

How do women now in business feel about preparation for business? What kind of preparation did they themselves have? I shall let them speak for themselves.

All four of my correspondents who confessed to less than high school education seem to have been successful in the work they are doing. (Perhaps the less successful ones did not write to me!) In any event, all four indicated that more education is desirable for women now entering business.

A Regina insurance underwriter who is a high school graduate says: "Everyone should have Grade 12. After that it depends on what a woman wants to do. University is okay but only to a certain extent. Many jobs don't require it. Training on the job is just as valuable."

A Charlottetown woman working in public relations is a registered nurse. She entered business by way of nursing, homemaking, and politics. She believes that a woman going into business benefits from a university education, and, she adds, "practical experience." Her business training had been taken, as had that of twenty-one of my correspondents, many years before at high school.

My correspondent who operates a private school for receptionists believes that the qualifications needed by a woman entering business depend on the business. "Formal training is not always necessary if one is an aware person, sensitive and suitable to one's chosen work. Work experience is, in the end, the best teacher."

Most working women, however, believe that formal education is important, and not merely for the reason given by the Alberta real estate agent, the building of confidence. Georgiana Evans, of Richmond, British Columbia, who is in banking, claims that a Bachelor of Arts degree is valuable, or better still a degree in Commerce or a master's degree in Business Administration, or all three. "Canadian business," she says, "places a high value on degrees and is willing to pay employees for them." The consensus is: Get as much education as you can. Decide on what you want to do and then get the training and the experience you need to do it as well as you possibly can. Nothing you learn about business, about people, about the special skills you need in your line of work is ever wasted. And finally, don't allow yourself to stay in a job where your training and expertise are not valued.

Most of the women who wrote to me had little time for membership in purely social clubs or organizations. What time they had to spare from their work and their families went to clubs of the service type and to professional organizations. The National Secretaries' Association, which sets international standards and examinations and issues certificates indicating that its members had passed the examinations and attained the standards, ranked high in the esteem of professional secretaries. I attended a meeting of the group in Winnipeg, spoke to two of its officers in Montreal, and have kept an alert eye open for its identifying pin wherever I go. There is no doubt that associations of this type do much to raise the prestige of businesswomen who think of their work in terms of career fulfilment. The associations serve the additional purpose of providing opportunities within their ranks for leadership training, for the promotion of communications skills, and for showing employers and the general public that businesswomen are serious about improving their performance and their image.

Repeatedly I heard this kind of comment:

Although some employers have a systematic pre-service training program for their employees – the department stores, for example – generally employers do not take enough responsibility for training their women employees. Often they do not see the women as needing additional training even when they complain about them not doing a good job. Sometimes they say loudly that they prefer to train their own people and want the people they hire to have only basic skills of reading, writing and arithmetic; but they do not follow through with systematic training programs. They leave the training to the girl-at-the-next-desk kind of thing. They rarely see their women employees as eligible for training for positions in the upper ranks of their companies. Well, maybe a little more than ten years ago, but not much more.

So you have your diploma from high school or business college or the community college, and you are ready to go to work in a store or an office or a bank or an insurance company. Will the fact that you are female stand you in good stead, or will you have handicaps to overcome because you are a woman?

4

Are Women Handicapped in Business?

The answer to that question depends a good deal on whom you ask. If you talk to Madame Queen Bee she will tell you that you will not have to surmount any hurdles that a man who is equally qualified would not have to conquer. Of course, she will tell you, not everyone makes good. You will need the special qualifications that she has. They enabled her to be successful, to handle a home and a husband and children and a full-time responsible position in business with the greatest of ease. *She* has had no trouble. If you have, it is obviously because you fall short of what's needed to be a womanly woman and a business success. Mme Queen Bee enjoys being unique, standing out from the crowd. She has no use for women's movements, and she does not particularly want your competition for her highly visible, highly enjoyable place in a man's world. Women disadvantaged? Nonsense! she will tell you. And if they are, it's their own fault.

If you ask Ms. Busy Bee she will give you a different answer. Sure, she will say, women are at a disadvantage in business, but it's usually their own fault. They can succeed if only they work 10 per cent harder than the men in their field, or twice as hard, or, if Ms. Busy Bee has been particularly frustrated on the day you approach her for advice, ten times as hard. But sure, you can make it. Well, perhaps not right to the top, not to the boss's rung on the ladder but to the place where you can hand him the hammer and the nails. You can be the world's best Girl Friday.

There are several incarnations of Ms. Busy Bee. One will urge you always to work hard and to remember that you are a lady; you will then be respected by both the women and the men you have to work with. Another will exhort you earnestly to work hard and cultivate, firmly and steadfastly, the qualities of ambition, single-mindedness, and aggressiveness, to forget you are a woman. A third will advise you that there is no conflict in being ambitious, single-minded, and aggressive, that energy and drive are not and have never been exclusively male characteristics.

Or you might ask Ms. Humble Bee. Her prototypes are numerous.

Her expectations of herself are low. She honestly believes that she cannot and should not aspire to positions of responsibility; she knows she's not good enough. "That's for the men," she'll tell you. She and her like form the sturdy backbone of the business world; they hold it up, but they do not know their own worth. Let me cite one instance.

Humble Bee is a lovely woman, lovely to look at and pleasant to talk with – she blushes when she has to disagree with anyone, no matter how mild the disagreement. She said to me as we walked out of a meeting we had both attended: "I didn't have anything to contribute to the discussion. Why should anyone want to listen to me? I'm doing the kind of work I know I can do. I admire you women who are aggressive" – she blushed when she called me aggressive, because in spite of her alleged admiration she considers the adjective derogatory when applied to a woman – "and have the push to get ahead. We should be grateful to you, but I couldn't do it." She will tell you that she has never felt at a disadvantage in her job because she is a woman. My guess is that she enjoys her humility; it gives her a well-defined place in life.

Ask Miss Worker Bee. "Of course there are disadvantages in being a woman at work. All sorts of them. I've lived with them all my life and expect to suffer from them after I retire on a pension (I'll be getting about a third of my immediate superior's). If I'd been a man he would have been working for me and not I for him all these years. But what can I do about it? I learned to accept these things long ago, and I am past fighting about it. But you, my dear . . ."

Or Miss Warrior Bee. She sees the barriers women have to scale in what she defines as a man's world. "But it doesn't have to be," she will say to you fiercely. "Change is coming and I am helping it along. Yes, I'll have to work twice as hard to get half the distance. Yes, there will be lots of people who will dislike me, or put me down; but there will be lots who will respect me. Sure there are disadvantages for a woman in business. Let's get moving and do something about removing them."

As a result of her study of 307 white-collar workers in British Columbia in 1969, M. Patricia Marchak wrote: "We found that regardless of education, women had less responsible and less authoritative positions than men; that regardless of job control level, they had less income than men. It didn't matter whether they were married or single, had no children or a family, had lengthy involvement in the labour force or very little experience, had university education or less than high school education, they were far more often to be found at the bottom of the promotion, skill, responsibility, and income scales than men."[1]

70

I asked women of every level of achievement, from every part of Canada, whether women at work had special difficulties to overcome, whether they believed themselves to be at a disadvantage, and if they did, what the disadvantage was. "Are you serious in asking that question?" one of my friends asked me. "Do you know how much money I am earning as compared with Jim Robinson? He's been with my company ten years less. We do just about the same job, but he's called an assistant manager and I don't have a title. I was hired as a stenographer seventeen years ago and haven't typed a letter in the last eight or ten, but I am still paid as if I were a stenographer. A senior one, for what that's worth. You want to know the major disadvantage we women suffer under? Salaries. Money, my dear friend, money. We don't make it."

We don't make it, in spite of human rights legislation and equal pay legislation. In fact, the gap between men's salaries and women's salaries seems to be widening rather than diminishing. Partly, Sylva Gelber says, because percentage increases in wages and salaries over the past inflationary years tend to give more money to the higher paid and less money to the lower paid. Since women are consistently the lower paid, the gap widens.

Madeleine Parent, vocal, dynamic secretary-treasurer of the Canadian Chemical and Textile Union, is only one of the many women who insist that so-called equal pay legislation has actually misled Canadian women. They believe what it says, and so think that they are protected from discrimination in pay. "What we need is not equal pay for equal work; that makes a good and convenient slogan. What we need is equal pay for work of equal value."

Women's work is almost totally undervalued: work at home, work at the office, work in the service industries, even volunteer work. As someone has remarked, when a man is co-opted to do a "volunteer" job, he becomes a dollar-a-year man. It is recognized that he gives up something of value – his time, his energy, his expertise – to do the job. When a woman does volunteer work it is considered to be her duty. She is making no sacrifice in giving time, energy, expertise because they are not important, command no price in the marketplace.

Moreover, job stereotyping has contributed to the inequity in payment. In spite of the women's movements, in spite of the publicity given to the stereotyping, in spite of the outlawing in many provinces of gender-oriented advertising, the number and percentage of women employed in the traditionally women's jobs have been steadily rising. In

1961, for example, women made up 63 per cent of the workers in white-collar jobs; by 1972 the percentage had risen to 72 per cent. By 1980, if present trends continue, it will be between 75 and 80 per cent.

Clerical jobs are notoriously underpaid as compared with other jobs because they are largely held by women. An interesting feature of such "women's" jobs is that the men who hold them are almost always better paid than their female counterparts.

According to Statistics Canada, the hourly earnings of full-time men employees in all small retail trade establishments exceeded those of women by 46.5 per cent. The largest gap between the hourly earnings of men and women was found in drug stores, where it was 90.3 per cent. In large retail establishments the drug departments also showed the greatest difference – 77.6 per cent.[2]

A Statistics Canada special survey of 350,000 employees of Canada's financial institutions, insurance, and real estate companies in October 1973 showed that in every occupational category the earnings of female employees were lower than those of males. Average weekly earnings that month were $113.21 for women and $207.88 for men. Women accounted for 55 per cent of all employees but only 6 per cent of the executives and 23 per cent of lower-level managers and supervisors.

A Canadian Press story from Vancouver, dated August 1, 1974, makes the statement that women are moving into jobs that were formerly classified as male, and it asks how many men are doing the reverse. Not many, it seems. "A check of Vancouver's six major banks showed a total of 1,700 tellers. None were men with the exception of male trainees who work at the position temporarily," the writer reported.

"Men aren't satisfied to remain as tellers," said one personnel representative. "Banks look for career people who will move on to management rather than people who will limit themselves to the lower salary of a teller."

Women, it seems, at least according to Vancouver bankers, are not interested in higher salaries or better positions.

Aren't they?

An article in the *Financial Post* of May 3, 1973, by John Davidson tells the tale of "Kathryn Ross," M.B.A., who applied for a job with a shoe importing company. One of the sales managers told Kathryn that he was looking for someone with experience to work with the company's foreign suppliers. "We talked about the job and my ideas seemed to coincide with what they were looking for. Then he asked me what kind of salary I was looking for. I said that I had in mind the going M.B.A.

72

rate – $9,000 to $13,000. He looked a little shocked and said that was a little higher than what they were prepared to offer me, say $130 a week. Here we had been discussing what seemed to be a responsible job that demanded certain specific qualifications I had and he was offering me $6,700 a year."

Kathryn suggested that $130 a week seemed a little low for the job, and he said that that was what they were paying all the girls around there.

Kathryn did not take the job.

Marilyn Cooper, a woman buyer in a large store, told me that she accepted her job knowing full well that she was being offered considerably less than her counterpart in an adjoining department. "But I felt that it was a breakthrough. There had never been a woman buyer in that department – carpets – before, and I wanted the job. I wanted desperately to prove that I could do it. I'm sure I'm good at it or I wouldn't have stayed. Our company isn't in business to be kind to its employees. I was told when I moved into the job that I could expect and would get no favours. But do you think I am making as much money as the men doing the same kind of work? No, ma'am, and I am not likely to be. When I pressed the point, I got evasion. When I went right to Mr. Number One on the matter, he looked at me kindly and said, 'Now look, my dear, you're a good girl and we appreciate you, but the men all have families to support. You have a perfectly good husband. You live well. What else do you want?' Imagine! In this day and age! I was furious. I reminded him that when I got the job it was on the basis of no favours. I thought the game should be played fair on both sides. He couldn't see it. I got a raise, but I am making less now than my predecessor got when he was moved to another position, and that's not taking inflation into account."

In the dim, unenlightened year of 1968 a Sault Ste Marie judge, passing judgement on a case brought by a policewoman for equal pay, is quoted as having said that "difference in wages is in accord with every rule of economics, civilization and family life, and is not discriminatory."[3]

The judge in 1968 and Marilyn's Number One man and the sales manager of the shoe importing company are not far apart in their thinking, in their attitudes to women's work and women's pay. The story is so familiar as to be trite. In these cases we were looking at inequities suffered by employed women, inequities that can be, or could be, removed by applying current labour, equal pay, and human rights legislation. "Current legislation, however, is not good enough at the federal level," Dr. Katie Cooke, then chairman of the Advisory Council on the Status of Women, has said repeatedly. "We'll keep on pressing the government to do better than make ineffectual promises for better human rights laws, and for their enforcement."

When she spoke with me in January, 1975, she had been suffering from a year and a half of frustration trying to convince the government that the time had come for action. "Not," said Dr. Cooke, "that legislation alone can erase all discrimination against women, but it does provide sanctions that can be exercised against those who deliberately discriminate." Furthermore, with legislation on the books frequently arrangements can be made out of court through the intervention of the appropriate agency under the sanction of the law. If the federal government would pass a law that forbade its agencies and departments to deal with companies that discriminated against women and would enforce the law, much of the discrimination would have to disappear.

But there are other kinds of inequities, the kinds that rise from the assumption that one kind of work (women's) is worth less than another kind of work (men's). Is the work of a young woman invoicing worth as much as or more than that of a young man meeting clients at a counter? Or is the differential in their pay based only on the fact that a woman is doing the one type of work and a man the other? Women are saying now that the value of work done should be assessed by criteria that are as objective as possible. There should be established for any work with a human factor (1) the skills required to perform the work; (2) the effort put into it, whether physical or mental; (3) the responsibility involved in it; (4) the conditions under which it is carried on; and (5), if applicable, the length of experience in it.

These criteria are neither new nor startling. They have been used in the construction of wage and salary schedules from the time such schedules were drafted. Professional and trades people are familiar with their application: a journeyman in a trade earns more than an apprentice, a surgeon with an established reputation for success in his or her field more than a colleague who is just beginning his or her career. The surgeon, moreover, can command a better salary and higher fees than the unskilled orderly in the wards or the handyman who tidies his garden. The heavy equipment operator on northern construction jobs may be paid a northern allowance to compensate for higher consumer prices and more difficult working conditions.

The system does not work perfectly, but it helps to establish some recognizable standards by which pay is determined; that is, when it is applied purely within the bounds of the male working world. Women are suggesting that similar guidelines be applied across the gender barrier, that an attempt be made to equate the value of work that is performed traditionally by women with the value of work that is performed traditionally by men: the truck driver and the sewing machine operator; the cashier and the "floor walker"; the woman who sells lingerie and the man who sells refrigerators.

So a major disadvantage faced by women in business is inequality of pay. Dr. Lynn McDonald, a Toronto sociologist, estimated the loss to Canadian women at seven billion dollars a year, a large portion of which is being lost by women working in offices, banks, retail and wholesale concerns, in business. No mean sum, and no wonder Canadian business, industry, and government shy away from the strong measures needed to remedy the situation.

Pensions. Pensions are tied to salaries, are in effect deferred salaries. Women who are disadvantaged because they are underpaid while they are actively employed suffer in greater proportion when they retire from work. They suffer, as many women told me with considerable bitterness, in many ways.

The most obvious is the smaller amount of their pensions. If they earn less, they receive less on retirement.

Worse, being office employees or sales people, many of them in small businesses without salary and fringe benefits negotiated in collective agreements, thousands of them have no pensions at all except for the Canada Pension and the Old Age Security payment. Nor, having earned poorly all their working lives, have they been able to accumulate much in the way of savings and thus find themselves in grinding poverty at the end of a working career of anywhere from twenty-five to forty-five years.

One old friend of mine, now retired, said to me with feeling, "Why, oh why did I decide to take a business course instead of Normal School when we both started out? You are going to be getting a healthy pension. You won't have to change your standard of living at all. Look at me. I've moved twice in the last couple of years because on my trickle of income I couldn't afford to pay the rising rents. I don't have a car. I pinch my pennies to be able to afford the things I think are important: visiting my family at the coast once a year, buying symphony and theatre tickets, having a friend in occasionally for lunch or dinner. Do you remember the novels we used to read when we were kids about the

English ladies living in genteel poverty? Let me tell you, there is nothing genteel about being poor. And at that I am better off than some of the women I know, widows who went back to work at fifty or fifty-five and saved nothing. How could they? We are not exactly starving, but life is a struggle."

Many women have broken service or have worked part time for many years. Few private pensions funds are portable, so that at retirement a woman can rarely count the pensionable years she had accumulated in the job she held before she was married; and part-time employees when – or if – they are permitted to pay into the pension fund accumulate very little equity. Moreover, even when a woman is allowed to vest the years she worked before marriage, the tendency (often on poor advice) when she leaves the job for marriage or child-raising is to withdraw her money. She thinks that she will never "work" again. How convenient to have the money right now to help buy a house or cover the cost of a new car! When she does return to work she may be too old to enter the company pension fund, or if she is allowed to pay into it the equity she can build up is small. Often she does not have the necessary years of service to be eligible for a reasonable pension when she does retire. Often she is forced by company policy to retire at sixty or sixty-five.

It is still common for pension funds to provide widow's survival benefits; a few now have spouse's survival benefits.

Where separate plans operate for management (male) and other employees (female), there are numerous plans that deny the same retirement benefits to women because they live longer. Plans such as these also often deny young women the right to join until they have had several years of service with the company, on the assumption that young women are not good tenure risks and are not interested in long-term benefits. Actually, of course, young men leave as frequently as young women. In the case of the women, however, the company has gained by not having paid in their portion of the pension during the first years of service: a clear gain for the company, a clear loss for the female employee.

Not unnaturally it is older women who mention inequities in pensions. Young women in their late teens and early twenties are not generally thinking in terms of retirement and pension. Nor, to be fair, are young unmarried men. At eighteen or twenty they are more concerned with the present than the immeasurably remote future.

Group insurance and salary continuation programs are frequently unfair to women, not merely in the benefits they offer, or fail to offer, but in the unjust assumption that young women are more likely to abuse them. Insurance plans of all kinds are geared to the family, and particularly to the family in which the man is the wage-earner. Dian Cohen, writing on "Women and Economic Discrimination – Insurance, a Problem" in 1974 has this to say: "A woman who supports herself, or her children, or whose income is necessary to her family's standard of living, faces financial disaster if disabling illness or accident prevents her from working. The gap between what men and women may obtain, and what premiums they pay is widest here."[4]

A survey carried out by the *Winnipeg Free Press* revealed that there was a great difference between what a man and a woman of the same age and occupation were being charged for the same coverage. It varied from company to company but always in favour of the man. An example: for a man and a woman, both thirty-seven years old, both professional economists, both presumably having the same income at the time of the inquiry, to provide a policy paying one thousand dollars a month to age sixty-five in the event of complete disability, one company would charge the woman $642.80 annually, the man $442.60, and another $685.00 and $440.00 respectively; a third would charge the woman $712.00 for coverage to age sixty-five, the man $514.00 for lifetime coverage. Still another company would give maximum coverage to the woman for five years only, though it would cover the man to age sixty-five.

All insurance companies excluded pregnancy as a cause of disability. At least two of the companies would pay only half-benefits to a woman unless her employment had been full time outside the home at the time of the onset of any disability. No such restriction was placed on a man. Most companies would not insure for disability a woman who worked at home, no matter what the work was. A typist making her living typing at home who lost her fingers in an accident? A consulting chemist working out of her residence? Neither would be eligible for disability insurance with most companies.[5]

Although men are more likely to suffer illnesses that require lengthy hospitalization – degenerative heart diseases, pneumonia, bronchitis, cirrhosis and other diseases of the liver – the myth persists that women are poor risks for salary continuance schemes and for disability insurance. Male patients with behavioural disorders also exceed female patients by 144 per cent. As Sylva Gelber caustically remarked, this last fact may account for the discriminatory rates set by the solely male officers of insurance companies.

So, women in business are often at a disadvantage as far as pension and insurance are concerned. Not all women, but many women.

It is not, however, in these cut-and-dried, easily documented areas that women have their greatest complaints to make. There they can see that changes can be made, by persuasion, by negotiation, by legislation. They find harder to prove and more difficult to deal with the often subtle, occasionally overt, discrimination they have found themselves subjected to in the matter of hiring and promotion, in day-by-day treatment; not always by men but by people.

Let me go back to Kathryn Ross and the article in the *Financial Post*. "Kathryn's first clue," John Davidson wrote, "that everything may not be out in the open when it comes to hiring women for management jobs, occurred when she applied for a position on the administrative side of one of the major airlines. Her application stated clearly that she was interested in an administrative job, nothing else. The personnel manager sat her down and began firing a battery of questions at her about such things as what her 'subservience quotient' was. After about an hour of give and take, when she figured she had made her qualifications and expectations quite clear, the interviewer asked her to stand up and turn around. After a good look he sat her down again and announced that there weren't too many administrative jobs open right then, but he would be pleased to offer her a job as a stewardess. Kathryn walked out, leaving him wondering what had gone wrong."

In 1975 all of the twelve labour jurisdictions in Canada, except the federal, Prince Edward Island, and the Yukon, prohibited discrimination in hiring on the basis of sex. Several have gone so far as to pass laws making it an offence to advertise jobs as specifically for men or for women, thereby giving great opportunity to humorists and cartoonists to exercise their wit.

It has not been too difficult to monitor the advertisements or to make changes in objectionable application forms, but attitudes change slowly and prejudices as deeply embedded in the culture as male-female images are hard to dig out. Kathleen Ruff, director of the British Columbia Human Rights Act, believes that progress is being made, though slowly.

She showed me examples of some of the old advertisements for jobs. In them were clearly revealed the expectations the advertiser had of the women he was going to hire, and of the men. The employment agencies detailed jobs for women under the heading "Career girls wanted!" The advertisements were what Kathleen Ruff called "gooey, juvenile, and adolescent in approach." The qualities listed were "charm" and "personality"; the adjectives used were "personable, attractive, pleasant." The advertisements for men, on the other hand, were for "Managers" and the qualities desired were "ability," "ambition," "aggressiveness." Even when the sex of the applicant was not mentioned the advertisements were clear in making known that men only need apply.

When the first furore died down – and it did not take long in those provinces that passed legislation banning sex discrimination in job advertising – it was amazing how quickly *sales people* replaced *salesmen* and *salesladies* in the Help Wanted columns, and how much more rational the advertising became.

Not entirely, of course. In a 1975 issue of a western daily I found the following advertisements under the heading "Office Help":

Recep.-Typist-P.T. Secretary $550 plus
Gal Friday, pleasant, attractive, nice personality. 2 yrs. office exp. to assist busy mgr. . . .

Secretary. Immed. opening for scrtry that likes a young progressive co. to work for. Shthd., dicta typing reqd. 3 years exp. essential. Personality and appearance impt. here. Excell. chance to prove your own initiative. . . .

Keypunch Operator $550 plus
Req'd. immed. acct. or typ. an asset. Familiar with 029, 3740, 3741, 3742 units. Must be able to work well around male oriented office. Call Kathy NOW! at. . . .

The first example is illegal in the province where it appeared. I am surprised that the employment agency placed it or the newspaper accepted it. In the others the sex orientation is not as obvious, and they might well slip by, although even the casual reader might wonder whom the receptionist-typist should be attracting and precisely what qualities Kathy had in mind for the keypunch operator who had to work well around a male-oriented office.

How much more to the point is an advertisement that appeared in the same context, and was, I am pleased to say, much more representative of the several columns of Office Help Wanted in the newspaper:

Leasing Person. Exp. person to do leasing and general office work in lge. apt.-hotel complex. Some typing needed. For interview call. . . .

We are so accustomed to filling in forms that we are not inclined to question what is on them. Yet application forms for jobs can work to the disadvantage of women. A woman in a supervisory capacity in a large company told me, "Our personnel officer did not discriminate against women; he simply laid aside applications from women for certain kinds of jobs that he had decided they were not suited for. The whole business of applications had to be forcefully brought to his attention, and not by us who work with him because he just paid no attention. So we sent one of our application forms to the chairman of a committee in our town who is working for the rights of women. She spoke to our head man and arranged a meeting with the personnel staff. I think she gave them some kind of test or questionnaire or something which they all discussed afterwards. I am not sure that our personnel man doesn't still set aside applications from women sight unseen, but he can't do it without a twinge of guilt and without being a little afraid of being caught doing it! Anyway, two changes have been made on the application forms. They now ask for first name or initials (so he can't tell on first glance whether the applicant is John or Joan). And the space for 'maiden name' has been eliminated! Yeah, a giant step forward for womankind."

In any event, in the provinces where discrimination in advertising and in hiring has been monitored by departments of labour or human rights bodies, most of the recent complaints have been regarding discrimination on the basis of sex. The complaints have been brought forward by women or on behalf of women who realized that they were being unfairly treated. Most cases have been settled informally and more or less amicably when they were brought to the attention of the offending companies. A few have gone to court and companies have been forced to eliminate formerly discriminatory practices.

Many incidents and situations, however, are never brought to anyone's attention. They remain unvoiced and unresolved. To have made a fuss about them would have been to invite unfavourable notice, and women have been conditioned to avoid that kind of thing. As one woman said, "So I would have won my point and soon afterwards when it was not too obvious, my job would have become – what do you call it? – redundant. What's the point in making a fuss? I've learned not to agonize over what I can't change." You will have recognized Miss Worker Bee in that remark.

I have already mentioned more than once the difficulties to be overcome by a woman who looks for promotion and the building of a career. These difficulties are encountered by both married and single women. Older married women reminded me that married women with working husbands are the most vulnerable during periods of high unemployment. "Do you remember," one of my contemporaries asked me, "the years when it was impossible for a married woman to hold a job, much less get one? Except doing housework, for next to nothing a day. I can see the same thing happening now. Unless we are on our guard the married woman will be the last to be hired and the first to be fired, regardless of how good she is. Deep down in their little hearts many men and more women than you would believe have the feeling that a woman should stay at home and be kept by her husband. Working, for her, is just an exercise to make her feel important. When times get tough the axe falls on the married woman first, on the older woman next, and finally on any woman, the theory being that a man is entitled to a job, but a woman gets one only when she is cheap to hire and is doing a job no man will take on."

My contemporary spoke from bitter and humiliating experience which the years have not erased. She added, "And don't think times have changed that much, or attitudes towards women working. When my daughter got married a couple of years ago, everyone, but everyone, asked her, 'Are you quitting your job?' or 'When are you quitting your job?' It made her furious. She has a better paying, a more responsible, and more interesting job than her husband's, but everyone expected her to give it up because she was getting married."

"This attitude to women working," my friend said, "is a greater handicap than anything else. It sets up all the other barriers."

Married women have also told me that there is a tendency on the part of many employers to think of them as part-time workers, even when they are full-time. Elizabeth, who has worked in one office or another for most of the twenty years of her marriage, believes that her employers never took her seriously or thought of her in any capacity other than the stenographic or clerical, although she was – and is – competent to do almost everything that her boss does. When an opening for a management position came along, she was called in and asked for suggestions. No one had thought of the possibility that she might be interested in the job herself. When she boldly said that she thought she could fill it, she was looked at as if she surely couldn't be serious about it. When she insisted that she was, her boss made a little joke and then said firmly that they had to be sure that anyone taking on the job would devote full time and energy to it. She had a husband. Suppose he were transferred? Besides, she couldn't go out with the boys in the evening. "You just wouldn't be comfortable," her boss said.

Elizabeth is not a fighter by nature. She didn't insist that she had the right to find out by trying whether or not she would be comfortable;

she caved in. "I suppose I should have resigned then and there," she said, "but I didn't. I'm still with the company, and still in the old job. Not that I don't enjoy doing it, but I must admit that I feel bitter every time the boy who filled the job I asked for has had a further promotion in the company" – a large construction outfit. She is what is called an office manager, but she does more than manage the office. "Our vice-president and general manager doesn't know as much about the ins and outs of the business as I do. He asks me when he has a decision to make. I suppose I am the power behind the throne. Not very satisfactory, because he earns at least three times as much as I do. I'm just the indispensable Mrs. So-and-so. I've wondered whether I would have been treated the same way if I had not had a husband on whom to blame the company's failure even to *see* me as a person of ability."

Marion, who is single, knows that the attribute of invisibility is not limited to married women. She has been in a position almost identical to Elizabeth's and has had proven to her, again and again, the fact that women are invisible to management.

Does the single woman have special problems, problems that differ from those of the married woman, or the "other" women, the sole-support mothers? Yes, and no, Marion says. "All women have to fight not only the social and economic set of business generally – the invisibility you talked about – they also have to fight both themselves and their employers because after all they have been thoroughly conditioned to think of themselves as lesser and less capable human beings. That's general for all women, married, single, widowed, divorced. Single women face other kinds of indignities because of what at least used to be the expectation that all women married, and if by chance any didn't, it was their fault.

"I can't tell you how sick and tired I still get – and I am forty – of being kidded about being an unclaimed treasure, or the comment that practically every single woman has had to listen to: 'I can't understand why a nice girl like you never got married.' "

Marion voiced the opinion of other single women in business when she remarked that it was hard for any employer to take a single woman's desire for a career seriously, at least until she was well past thirty. It is assumed when a young man enters the service of a bank, for instance, that he is thinking in terms of banking as a career. It is assumed when a young woman enters the service of a bank that she will work until she is married, or after marriage until she is pregnant. In spite of recent consciousness – and conscience – regarding the promotion of women in the banks, very few women have been made bank managers and almost all of these in small residential-area banks. Marion is angry about that fact but almost as angry with her female colleagues, in banks and elsewhere. She showed me a clipping from a daily paper. A newly appointed woman bank manager was asked by a reporter whether she thought of banking as a lifetime career. Marion and I could almost hear the simper in her voice when she said, or was quoted as saying, "I'll have to decide on that later. I suppose if I met the right man I might want to settle down as a wife and mother . . ." or words to that effect.

"That kind of woman annoys me no end," Marion said in exasperation. "She undermines my position and that of every woman who does think of her work in terms of a career. She annoys me, and so does the reporter. Can you imagine him (or her) asking a newly appointed male manager the question in expectation of the same kind of answer? Well, I suppose the reporter asks the questions he thinks will bring newsworthy answers. But what's newsworthy about that woman's answer? You hear it all the time. You'd think we have enough difficulties to overcome without us women aggravating them."

Women are further handicapped in their struggle for upward mobility – or so we are told – because they are less likely to be geographically mobile than equally ambitious males.

Many, perhaps most, national and international companies train their executives by moving them around the country, or, at one stage of development, around the world. This policy can be highly discriminatory to working women in two ways. On the one hand, married women whose husbands are eligible for transfers force their husbands to make difficult decisions or more frequently find that there are no decisions to make. The husbands' careers come before the wives'. Women with executive potential are often passed over by their employers on the grounds that there is no point in training them; just as they are ready for a position of responsibility they leave because their husbands are transferred. On the other hand, married women, and single women with elderly parents or other dependants are often in a position where they are themselves not free to be moved from city to city in order to further their careers. It is true that in some families husbands and wives can rationally discuss the relative importance to the family and to themselves as individuals of the wife's job and the husband's and do sometimes come to the conclusion that it is in the best interests of all for the family to move when the wife has an opportunity for promotion by moving to another city. If, however, I am to believe most of the women I have questioned, the husband's job still takes precedence in most households. The wife's is secondary, and she is usually not free to move.

The policy of moving executives-in-training unquestionably needs re-examination. Men as well as women are questioning its validity and the upheaval it causes in their lives and in the lives of their families.

An executive officer of a large national company, with many branch offices from coast to coast, told me that he personally thinks the business of transferring bright young men from city to city is a lot of nonsense. "My family and I both suffered as a result of that policy," he said to me. "My second son attended five different schools between the ages of five and eleven. It was rough on my wife, too. She made no real friends during the years when friendships are so important. The policy made our lives superficial, and I can't believe that it helped me know more about our company's business than if I had been allowed to learn the operation of my home branch thoroughly or been moved, say, once in ten years. I'm certainly giving the matter serious thought, and so are some of our other top men. We all need roots, and none of us have them."

Several of the women I talked to about the policy of training executives through mobility believed that the policy could be and frequently was used as an excuse for not giving women opportunities for job diversification and promotion. They noted, with bitterness, that young men who resisted moves on personal grounds still were able to reach managerial positions whereas women were never offered the positions in the first place. When I posed the question to the executive officer, he thought for a moment, and replied that he didn't think the policy was used as an excuse. "I am embarrassed to admit that we men don't need an excuse for not promoting women within our companies. We just don't do it, and that's that."

Perhaps they don't do it because they enjoy thinking of women as "less capable and lesser human beings," to use Marion's term; perhaps because women outside their "natural" role make them uneasy; perhaps because they are afraid of the competition; perhaps because they have never lived or worked in an environment where women were not considered "less capable and lesser human beings." Whatever the reasons, women like Marion have found themselves, and have resented, being thought of and treated like lesser human beings.

V. E. Morrison is office manager and assistant to the vice-president of her Ontario-based firm. Her duties include financing, job costing, taking part in company policy making, and yet she says, "The difficulties

I have encountered as a woman in business have been mainly with male peers. They do not like to be confronted by a female on matters of administrative procedure, and often appear to resent any discussion with me on administrative matters."

Jean MacDonald of Westmount, Quebec, is in real estate, a field that has become increasingly attractive to women. She says, however, that "some businessmen are frightened of capable women and resent having them in positions of influence."

Erika Hamel, assistant manager in a trust company office, in her middle twenties, says, "There are times when customers wanting financial advice completely refuse to speak to me. Their response is, 'No, dear, I want to speak to someone who knows.' When I explain that I am able to help them, they still insist on waiting for a man to talk to. (It's not my youth, because the man they talk to is about the same age.) Another problem for a woman is the pressure on her to prove that she can do the job. A man does not have the same need to prove his ability. He already has his credentials; he is a man."

Several other women echoed Erika's last comment. There is great pressure on women to prove themselves in jobs other than those they are expected to fill. Men too are subject to the pressures of proving themselves, but many women, like Erika, insist that they have an additional load because of the scepticism that surrounds them simply because they are female.

Louise Hardy, who is, or was when I spoke with her, co-ordinator of women's programs for Canada Manpower in Montreal, made an interesting point about the position of women in the province of Quebec. Quebec men, she said, perceive women as ruling the country through the home, in the schools. They don't want a woman boss in the office. There has therefore been little improvement of women's position in business. There are competent, indeed excellent, token women, but they remain token women. The pressure – and here she agrees with Erika – on women to succeed in these token jobs is almost overpowering. "If I lose," the woman thinks to herself, "I will let all women down." Ms. Hardy does not believe that the situation in Quebec is really much different from that in the other provinces, except perhaps more noticeable. As in other jurisdictions, what happens is not the result of legal sanctions but of cultural imprints.

Not all women see themselves as being at a disadvantage, and some who do place the blame almost wholly on themselves. "If there are any disadvantages, they are probably my own fault."

Frequently even women who gave a negative answer to the question, "Have you encountered difficulties as a woman in business that a man might not have had?" in their other comments identified some difficulties. Moyra Roberts, stockbroker, Vancouver, twenty years in the working world, answered the question with "Not really." Then she went on to say that what a woman needed to succeed in business was "Guts – more guts, and possibly a sugar daddy! Determination and aggression, qualities necessary for men and women." Women, she believes, hold few positions of influence in the business world because of "prejudice – of men to women *and* women to women." Then there is domestic interference. "Most of us lose ten vital years in marriage and child-bearing."

Helen L. Young, systems representative in the design and sale of accounting and statistical systems, is a widow without dependants living in Edmonton. Asked about difficulties, she answered, "No, not to my knowledge. I suppose it is possible that an occasional lost sale may have been one which went to a competing company because the sales representative was a male." She gives three reasons why women do not advance to positions of authority:

- Both men and women have expected that women will advance along a horizontal plane – that is, moving to better salary within an area traditionally considered to be work for women – but have not thought of women moving upward into influential positions.

- Women have not helped other women with encouragement and co-operation in job situations.

- Women have generally lacked the confidence to move upward in management and therefore did not become conditioned to the idea or educated for it.

Once more I detect an underlying awareness of difficulties faced uniquely by women, although Mrs. Young's answer to the specific question was "No, not to my knowledge." There is a similar awareness in what Anne-Laure Levain of Montreal said. Mme Levain came to Canada from Belgium in 1951, speaks five languages, and is now administrative director of a biochemical laboratory. She believes that there are neither advantages nor disadvantages for a woman in business but adds the comment that "we are a bit under pressure at times when having to cook and take care of family problems *after* work. A man would not have these extra problems."

Her response was typical. It came in one form or another from single, widowed, divorced, and married women. What was noticeable and notable was how many of the women giving it tacitly accepted their dual role, their total responsibility for running the home. There were, of course, also women who talked about the sharing of family responsibilities and household tasks, but among my correspondents they were in the minority. For most it was an immutable fact of life, not to be questioned, that the wife and mother had primary responsibility – or total responsibility – for homemaking.

The plight of the woman who is associated with her husband in a small business is inextricably bound to the theory that the wife is an extension of her husband, without individual rights – or with few individual rights – of her own. Court decisions dealing with a woman's right to a substantial property accumulated during her marriage upheld the theory in law as in tradition. The recommendations flowing from Crossroads '75, a conference sponsored by the International Women's Year Secretariat and the Quebec Status of Women Council, reflect accurately the concerns of Quebec women and the problems that confront women who share in the building of a business, often without pay because their husbands cannot claim their salaries as legitimate income tax deductions.

The conference recommended:

- That a wife who is an associate of her husband in a small business should be recognized as an active member of the labour force provided she meets certain criteria: the contribution of minimum hours of work and the sharing of responsibility (that is, the criteria for partnership in a business enterprise), although the wife may not have made a cash investment. Presumably her labour has been the equivalent of capital.

- That when a family business is converted into a company, the wife's previous unpaid participation in the business should be assessed and legally recognized; in addition this assessment should be converted into shares in the company.

- That when a business with a sole owner is converted into a company whose shareholders are members of the immediate family, that is, spouse and children, sales taxes should not apply on the value of the transferred property.

- That pressure should be brought to bear on the federal and provincial governments to remove the section of the income tax laws forbidding the husband who is "sole or joint owner" from deducting from his income as an operating expense the salary paid to his "wife/employee." This would make it possible for the working wife to receive a salary in the same way as any regular worker.

- That a wife who meets the criteria of associate of a sole owner, even if she has no income of her own, should be allowed to join the (Canada) pension plan by paying minimal premiums or having her husband pay these premiums on her behalf.
- That the law should be amended to allow a wife who is the associate of a majority owner to claim unemployment insurance benefits.[6]

The substance of these recommendations has been enunciated by women's groups in the other provinces of Canada, particularly those recommendations pertaining to inequities in federal legislation. Although many women find themselves in the situations that the women attending Crossroads '75 wished to change, none of the women who corresponded with me mentioned the inequities set forth in the recommendations, probably because most of them were engaged in businesses independent of their husbands'. Moreover, women who have a successful marriage and who work side by side with their husbands rarely think of themselves as being financial partners; they feel the business is mutually theirs and they think of themselves as a unit, not as the lesser of two parts. It is only when the marriage breaks down, and a settlement has to be made, that the wife realizes that her years of devotion and the major contribution she has made to the building up of the business can be utterly meaningless.

As this is being written the precedents being established in law are still ambivalent regarding a woman's rights in property to the growth or development of which she has contributed through her work. On the other hand, courts tend to rule in her favour when she has made a contribution of money to the business. That condition says something about the status of the married woman who works side by side with her husband.

Self-employed women are on the whole confident, interested in their work, and closer in attitude to the Queen Bee than to the Humble Bee.

When they mention difficulties to be overcome by women, the obtaining of credit is high on the list: "I am president and majority shareholder in the company, and so can be said to be self-employed. The self-employed woman does encounter some obstacles in obtaining capital to either start or purchase a business. Very often financing can only be obtained if her husband or a businessman is willing to back her. It also is of benefit to have established businessmen on the company board of directors."

From Vancouver, Reva Lander, consultant, R. Lander and Associates Limited, answered the question regarding difficulties specific to women: "Only in relation to financing."

From Lake Cowichan, British Columbia, Dorothy Clode sent the word: "Mortgages are difficult to get. You almost have to have a male partner or male underwriters."

From Toronto, Susan Cooke, president of Comar Management Services Incorporated: "Yes, I would say that a self-employed woman is handicapped, especially in my field, not so much in getting credit, making contacts, or obtaining capital but perhaps in trying to sell your abilities and know-how in a man's world. From my own point of view it appears that many of the old-guard type men tend not to listen. . . . Ideas [from women] tend to be pooh-poohed only to be used later with no credit or financial recognition given to the woman who suggested the ideas in the first place."

In Summerside, Prince Edward Island, Frances Perry took over the family business, a motion picture theatre, when she inherited it from her brother. With the help of her husband she has built it into a flourishing and diversified operation. She wrote: "I am self-employed, president of our company, and main decision-maker. I have no trouble obtaining capital because of my inheritance. (I already had the money I needed.) I have encountered no difficulties simply because I have worked harder than any man. . . . A woman needs to have the stamina of two men to succeed and a great need of diplomacy." Mrs. Perry added her voice to the call for more women to help women. "Other women must encourage women to get ahead. A closer relationship with all women should help." She also pays tribute to the support of "an excellent husband and family. Without them I could not have functioned so well."

Alma Lorelei Meis's training is in home economics. She also took the Small Business Management course at Southern Alberta Institute of Technology and formed her own company, Calgary Consulting Home Economists Limited. She wrote: "The greatest handicap [a self-employed woman faces] seems to be her own inexperience. Time is wasted in accomplishing anything at all, in obtaining capital, etc. You get answers if you know the questions, but it takes time to learn what questions to ask. Then whom does one approach? Speaking personally, I was divorced, and so had some trouble with the bank initially."

A frequent comment was that women have difficulty meeting the people they should know because they do not have the same informal avenues for socializing. Anne Willoughby Shepherd operates an art studio in Medicine Hat, Alberta. "I am," she wrote, "now self-employed. I have not had a need to obtain extra capital or to establish credit; however, making contacts is something else again. . . . My work is of the kind that few men in the same field wish to compete in, just as I have no wish to do huge banners, scaffold work, etc. I think men do have more opportunity to make business connections than women do at present."

Businessmen see one another over lunch at the weekly or monthly service club meetings, Rotary, Kiwanis, Lions, Kinsmen. Women are excluded. "I have neither the time nor the interest to be a Ladies' Auxiliary member, or whatever it's called," one busy young woman said. "Besides, I have almost nothing in common with the women who come together because their husbands happen to have a community of interest."

There are several women's clubs that to some degree parallel male service clubs. They serve a purpose in that they provide opportunities for women to exercise leadership and to accept responsibility as office holders. They also bring together and establish relationships among women of like interests in business and the professions. Unfortunately they have neither the power nor the prestige of their male counterparts, since so few of their members occupy seats of authority. As long as business remains a predominantly male domain, the female service clubs will isolate their members and will not establish a broad base for social and business contacts with their peers, colleagues, and rivals.

Marion, whom I have already quoted, is vehement on the subject. "It's not that I particularly want to go out with the boys for a drink, but the fact remains that an awful lot goes on between people when they are having a coffee or a drink together. Relationships valuable to business are begun and established through these contacts. Single women are in a particularly vulnerable position. We find it hard to ask a guy out for a drink or even for lunch – though I think that's changing. (Expense accounts help. Guys don't mind a woman paying for their lunch when it is understood that it's really the company paying and not the woman!) Anyway, maybe because I am forty and fairly well established it is becoming possible for me to invite a business associate or a customer out for lunch or for a drink. I am reaching the stage where I can entertain at home, too, though I have to be careful about whom, how many, and so on. What's even more important, when I was younger it would have been awkward for my boss to take me out for lunch or for a drink, or to take me along on a business conference, without snide comments being made or sidelong looks. You know the sort of thing. I don't think things have changed very much."

Evelyn MacLachlan, truly a woman in a traditionally male field – she is a reinforcing steel consultant – wrote: "I have found as a self-employed woman that I have no more difficulty than men in obtaining capital or establishing credit, but making contacts is easier for men, I think, as some that you meet do not seem to think the place for women is dealing in business." Mrs. MacLachlan thinks that women are handicapped in social ways. "If you are trying to butter up a contractor or a bank manager or have a bit of trouble on a job, if you are a man you can ask these people to go to lunch, or go to a hockey game, or play eighteen holes of golf, or what have you. As a woman I find this impossible."

Though women are acutely aware of the difficulties they face in making their way in business, some of them are convinced that they have had advantages because of their femaleness. Others believe strongly that there is no difference, that men and women compete on equal terms, and that is the way it should be. Greta Hale is one of them. She was the first woman elected president of the Bakery Council of Canada. She had learned the family business from the ground up, having begun as a cookie packer at thirteen and served at catering jobs on Saturdays. She claims that she has not been handicapped as a woman in business, although she has had family responsibilities. Acceptance of them has meant working harder – as it would have for a man in the same position – "getting up earlier, working longer hours, putting aside some of the outside interests I might like to take on. . . . However, there is no area of business where women with ability and training cannot enter and succeed. . . . My father says cream always rises to the top. And so it is with women who enter the business world to serve."

Jean Tweed of Toronto has had a varied career and came late, and, as she says, "by chance," into business. She is well known as a writer, editor, and broadcaster. She has served as business manager for an artists' union and farmed for eight years. "I have never been handicapped by being a woman. I like it. I probably had less difficulty than a man might have had. I had a brilliant husband, a wealthy father, good health, and some brains of my own."

"A brilliant husband, a wealthy father. . . ."

Another woman wrote: "Yes, there are many advantages in being a woman. Not the least of them is having a husband you can fall back on, belonging to the right family, the right social group. It didn't do me any harm to have gone to the right girls' school, and danced with the boys at the right boys' school. I am sure it was easier for me to get a job when I was widowed at forty because I knew the right people and to get credit when I wanted to start a business at forty-five for the same reason. Maybe you can't count these as particularly female advantages. I think they are. A man who hadn't 'worked' before forty would never have got anywhere near where I did."

Still another woman, who also preferred to remain anonymous, said quite frankly, "I use my feminine wiles just as a man uses his masculine attributes. I dress well, I use good perfume, I have my hair done regularly. I bat my eyelashes when I think the man I am dealing with is susceptible to that kind of treatment. Sure, I have advantages."

"Not the least of the advantages," one canny businesswoman told me, "is that men don't expect us to be able to do anything in their line. So they are not as much on their guard with us. They can be more open." And another added, "Besides, there are the fringe benefits conferred by some of the male chauvinists who feel that they should assist and be helpful because we are female. They can be very pleasant and encouraging."

As Barbara Scott and several other people pointed out, these benefits are ephemeral and in the long run insignificant. They consist of having doors opened, chairs held at the table, of being helped on with a coat, the traditional little courtesies.

Or, as someone else put it, "There may be certain advantages in being a woman in the business world, but that would be more on a person-to-person basis, and I don't believe that would count as far as advancement or achievement or recognition is concerned. By advantages I mean they, that is, women, are extended courtesies that a man might not receive."

Being unique, being a woman in a predominantly male field, can be an advantage. A tax expert said she had a card printed, using only the initials of her first names. Only her initials appeared on her letterhead. When she walked into an office, or a client walked into her office, the element of surprise proved an asset. No one expected her to be female. Once she entered into discussion of her subject, any problems that might have arisen vanished because the client was immediately aware that she knew what she was talking about.

A woman with many years of work experience behind her told me that a cardinal rule of her dealings with men was always to remember that she was a lady. "When a woman acts like a lady she is treated like a lady. I find that men – and women too – are uniformly polite to me when I am myself, acting as I was brought up to act. I've seen too many women trying to be like men. I find them distasteful." Her ladylike upper lip lifted slightly to indicate just how distasteful.

She has many supporters. Lila has worked with men all her life; she and her husband were in the trucking business, hauling gravel and building roads. Never, she said, had she found it necessary to be anything but womanly, no matter how rough the work, how masculine the clothing, how difficult the working conditions. "I respected the men, and they respected me for what we could both do equally well. I didn't have to be rough, tough, and nasty to prove that I knew the job. In fact, it helped to be a woman."

And men who work with or employ women, what is their reaction? My sampling is smaller, but it provides a range of opinion.

"Women take advantage of being women," said one male employer. "Okay, so they do a good job, but – and it's a big but to me – every time their kid sneezes they stay home to look after it. Where would my business be if I did that? They expect to be treated on equal terms with the men in the office, but if you ask them to stay to finish a piece of work they always have an excuse – like their husbands don't want them to work overtime or they have to get home to make supper for their husbands and kids. Another thing I might mention since we are on the subject, will you tell me why women expect to be *asked* if they want a promotion? A man has to get out there and fight for it, but the woman, for God's sake, yacks because no one asks her to take a job."

When I respectfully suggested to him that he was not talking about advantages that women had, but – if he was right – disabilities they had to overcome, he snorted and muttered that that's the trouble with women; they never can discuss anything rationally. It always gets twisted.

Other employers, male and female, were more positive, if equally brainwashed. "Women are very good at certain kinds of work, detail work. They enjoy doing anything that requires great care and attention, where men tend to be slapdash."

And: "I'll never employ a man to do my books again, not after my excellent experience with my last two bookkeepers, both women. Too bad one left to have a baby and the other one's husband was transferred."

And: "I've always enjoyed working with women. They are conscientious; they don't expect too much; in all the years I've never met one who was an alcoholic. (I wish I could say the same for the men.) As far as I am concerned, yes, there is an advantage in their being female. For certain kinds of work, of course." This from a hospital administrator.

"If I can have brains and beauty in one lovely person, I'll opt for her every time. I like to have good-looking gals around; they make a good impression, on me as well as my clients," another man said to me. "Especially the beauty," he added.

I barely restrained myself from retorting, "Right. Next time I interview a male teacher for a job, I must remember to put more emphasis on his handsome face and burly figure than on his ability to teach."

"Somehow the whole atmosphere of a place changes because one of the girls has brought in a bowl of flowers from her garden; or the girls are having a shower for someone who is leaving to get married; or birthdays are remembered. Those are the kinds of things women do as a matter of course. They remind me that the human touch – the woman's touch, if you want to be chauvinistic about it – can do more to make a place run smoothly and to turn out good work than all the efficiency experts," the owner of a small manufacturing plant said to me. "Not that some of the gals in top jobs aren't plenty ruthless."

More than once I was told that women have an advantage in being good negotiators and conciliators. From birth they have been conditioned to getting what they want by negotiation and conciliation rather than confrontation. "We can help tempers from flaring up," one of them said to me. "For one thing men still try to control themselves a little more when there are women around; the atmosphere is less brutal, shall I say? Or at least that's what my colleagues tell me. In all seriousness, though, we women have been used to conciliating, to keeping the peace. I think everything we have been brought up to be has taught us the value of compromise and conciliation and, yes, diplomacy. We've been used to yielding gracefully. There are times in business when that's a very useful kind of attribute to have and to share: to be able to compromise, to give way with good grace and without losing face."

A man put it a little differently. "You women," he said to me, partly with exasperation and partly with genuine admiration, "are able to get your own way by seeming to give us ours. Maybe it's me, but I have sure been outmanoeuvred more than once by a couple of very bright young ladies. It wasn't until much after the event that I realized what had happened. While they had given in on a few minor points I had yielded a major point. I must admit to you that I would have felt much worse about it if the deal on their terms hadn't turned out better than I had expected for both of us. It's what is called twisting a man around your little finger, and making him like it."

The stereotypes in women's minds were no less evident than in men's. "Women are more understanding; they are more sympathetic; they are more humane; they are not as pushy." All the "feminine" qualities inferred in the adjectives were cited as advantageous to women in business.

- "Real estate is a natural for women. They know what other women want and need in a home."
- "We're good at detail work. We're more careful than men."
- "Women work harder."
- "They don't want responsibility at work."
- "There are all kinds of things men do better. Why don't we leave those things to them and concentrate on what we can do well?"
- "A job must always remain secondary to a woman while it comes first with a man."
- "Concerns for people go deeper because most women have a natural mothering instinct."

J.J. is a man who has worked with women and has had women working with him all his life. He summed up much of what I heard both men and women saying with considerable frequency. "I've worked with all kinds of women. With the best of them we were both able on the job to forget that there was any difference in sex, without – and this is important – the women trying to pretend that they were men. Off the job we have always done a lot of good-natured kibitzing and kidding around about women's rights and all that stuff. I don't know," he said, "which is more objectionable, the girl who wants to be one of the boys and tries to out-cuss and out-drink them, or the girl who is giggly girly and hanging around trying to be noticed. Thank God, I haven't had to put up very long with either kind. Most of our women are here to do a job as well as they can and it doesn't matter to them or to us whether they are doing it with men or with other women."

The conclusion to be drawn from all this seems to be that women are at a disadvantage in the business world. Not all women, of course. Those of us who have the initial advantage of family support, education, some capital have a better chance of becoming successful in what is a competitive establishment. Those of us who set out on our careers without the initial advantages face a double handicap; being a woman is probably the greater part of it. Self-employed women, on the whole, have a better time of it than employed women, although they suffer from difficulty in obtaining credit and insurance and in making business contacts because of their femaleness. Employed women, in spite of equal pay legislation, are still substantially underpaid as compared with their male counterparts and are discriminated against in the matter of pensions and insurance – group, disability, and life. Hiring practices militate against them, and there are vast injustices in the promotion policies of most businesses.

And always there are the myths of what is woman's work, what a woman's place is in the world. Not all the fault lies with the employers; often women themselves are to blame for the disadvantages they face. Their own ideas of what they can or cannot, should or should not, do handicap them in the struggle for advancement, indeed, leave them out of the struggle entirely.

The picture is not all dark. Although progress is slow, attitudes are changing, official attitudes especially. Human rights legislation and human rights commissions, as well as equal pay and other anti-discriminatory legislation are having some effect. There is also a growing awareness of the right of women to self-realization in whatever field of endeavour they decide they want to try and a growing militancy on the part of groups of women.

Moreover, women themselves, and the men they so often work for, are beginning to understand that qualities usually described as "feminine" are human and humane and are not inimical to "success" in business or any other walk of life. The ability to admit a mistake, the ability to yield without a loss of face, the ability to conciliate differences – these qualities in man or woman if given greater scope would create an environment more conducive to sound mental health than the embattled setting in which many highly competitive businesses now operate.

Most important, more women are beginning to think of possibilities for advancement in business in untraditional fields and are taking active measures to prepare themselves for new roles, self-confidently and un-self-consciously. They recognize the disadvantages under which women currently labour and are determined through their own efforts, example, and support for other women not merely to overcome the disadvantages but to wipe them out.

Most of us from time to time have wakened in the morning and thought to ourselves, "No, I can't. I simply can't face another day of this." Then we get up, get dressed, and go off to work. Moreover, not only do we face the day but on counting our blessings we discover that the job which loaded so many frustrations on us also provided considerable satisfaction.

Frustration and Satisfaction

I asked women in business what most frustrated them in their work and what gave them particular satisfaction. Not, I made clear, the major disadvantages or advantages that we had previously discussed but the day-by-day frustrations and satisfactions that make life either difficult or pleasant. As with any consideration of human behaviour and human perception, there were both unanimity and diversity in the replies I received.

To me it was interesting that not one of the women with whom I spoke or corresponded volunteered as an annoying or frustrating element of her job something that came to the fore quickly and repeatedly when I asked a direct question about it. Maybe women have come to expect a certain amount of minor sexual harassment without protest; maybe some women are conditioned to accept it as a form of compliment; maybe they are embarrassed to discuss it because they feel that they have in some way provoked it and are therefore to blame. Anyway, I heard about the problem only after I asked about it.

Harriet is a young woman who might have answered the advertisement for a "personable typist." "Yes," she said in reply to my question as to whether she had suffered any unpleasantness related to sex. "Do you know what annoys me around the office, or at least has annoyed me occasionally? In fact, upset me badly. It's exactly that – sex. I don't mean just being a woman; that I like and enjoy, but being bothered by men because I am a woman. I was pretty young when I got my first job. It was in a small office, and there were many times when I was alone with one of the men, an older man, I am sure older than my father. He was a very respectable man as far as anyone knew, but the moment we were alone he would come over and sort of push me, if you know what I mean. He would put his hand on me, or his arm around my shoulder, and once or twice he tried to go further. I was scared and embarrassed and didn't know how to handle the situation. I wondered what I was doing to make him think he could treat me as he tried to. Of course I wasn't doing anything. I was just female. It made me – *me*, for heaven's sake – it made *me* feel dirty. I couldn't tell anyone at home, and I was too shy to talk about it to anyone else. So I tried to avoid him."

How had she finally solved the problem? "Well, one day I just got mad and yelled at him to leave me alone. Someone came into the office at that moment. The fellow thought the man who'd come in had heard or seen something and left in a hurry. I never had any more trouble with him, but I always felt he was out to get me. I left as soon as I could find another job."

Harriet did not realize how many women had had similar experiences. "There are several kinds of male nuisances," a smart young office worker said. "The middle-aged or elderly pawing types. They are disgusting. Most of them have wives and live respectably hypocritical lives but can't keep their hands off any girl they are near, in a sneaky, unpleasant way. Then there are the jocks – young or old – who think that every girl is dying to fall into their arms. They're not hard to handle. You just put them in their place. And there are the smoothies, the out-of-town sharp guys. They give you the business about how lonesome their lives are when they are on the road. They butter you up, ask you out for dinner, and invite you up to the room for a drink either before or after dinner. If you go you're fair game because they think that you know what to expect and would be disappointed if they didn't live up to your expectations. They're not hard to handle either. They like to boast about their conquests, but they're pretty cagy just the same; they want fun but no trouble. Don't get me wrong. They'll try and try hard, but if you fall for them it's your own fault."

"The temptations of the road aren't limited to the men," said a woman who travels a good deal for her company and takes in two large conventions a year, one in Canada and one in the United States. "If you are an unattached woman and want sex, it's not hard to find. I could tell you a couple of hairy tales about things that happened to girls, or nearly happened, just because they were on the scene. Women's lib or no, women are still pretty vulnerable in certain situations. Most of us can take care of ourselves. We've been around long enough to know what's what. And most of the men are decent fellows, out to have a good time and meaning no harm. Personally, I have always been well treated, but then I don't leave myself open to trouble. I've seen plenty of women who were the aggressors sexually, too."

"Has anyone talked to you about the relationship that sometimes develops between a man and his personal secretary?" Marion asked me.

"In many cases there are strong sexual overtones there. I don't mean sleeping together. I know of cases where the secretary never addressed her boss as anything but Mr. So-and-So, but the role she filled was that of wife and mother combined. The yearning, unexpressed even to herself, for something more was clear as crystal to everyone but to her and her boss. Offices where that kind of relationship exists generally are not good for other women to work in. It's a sort of sexual exclusion, a possessive jealousy. In those situations the secretary and others in the office both suffer from all kinds of frustrations, and you have petty explosions."

What about the trite plots in which the man's secretary comes between him and his wife? Does that happen very often?

Not really, I was told. Sure, young women and young men meet and fall in love when they work together, and occasionally there is the Cinderella story of the girl who marries her boss. Sure, very occasionally you hear of a broken marriage after which the boss marries his secretary. But generally speaking men and women work together as colleagues. A good friend of mine informed me that the last person a secretary wants to marry is her boss. She knows him too well. There is not much romantic glamour to him after they have worked together for any length of time. They have a relationship; if it is a good one, there is mutual respect and liking. "That's all," she said. "If a sensible girl finds she is becoming just a little too interested in her boss, and the boss is married – and even if he isn't – she waves good-bye and finds another place to work. Sex and business don't mix."

But it is there in one or other of its manifestations, as I discovered when I asked about it, and in some of its forms it creates frustrations that can be resolved only by leaving the job.

One of its manifestations that is difficult to fight is sex-based humour.

Not long ago I was waiting at a repair shop for my car. The proprietor asked me whether I liked jokes, and when I said I did, he handed me an automotive magazine. On the last page was the usual collection of the jokes that appear in automotive magazines and other magazines devoted to the male trades. Of twelve inane jokes, ten were at the expense of women, some of them anatomical. The fighting feminists among businesswomen have been irked by this kind of humour and find themselves battling it with minimal success. Nothing is harder to combat than the good-natured joke, as thousands of women have found.

"I protest the sexist humour on general principles," one bright young thing said to me seriously. "Around the office everyone thinks I have no sense of humour because I take everything that's said dead seriously and try to point out how much harm those stupid comments can do and how they reveal deep-seated anti-female attitudes."

I can imagine the reaction she gets and how carefully she will be avoided after a while as a bore and a spoilsport – that is, after the office wags have tired of leading her on to justified indignation.

The wall of the little repair shop where I called for my vacuum cleaner was plastered with cartoons of large-bosomed females bursting out of their bodices and leering males making appropriately obscene remarks. The pale thin young woman at the desk glanced at them when I made a comment about them and said, "I don't even see them. Some of the customers kid me about them, and I just look them – the customer, I mean – straight in the eye and don't say anything. I guess they expect me to laugh, but why should I? The boys in the shop keep changing them."

"I don't mind the cartoons, or even the dirty jokes. I don't have to look or listen. What gets me down is the complete insensitivity of some people. They can be downright vicious when they feel threatened as so many men seem to by the women's movement. When you try to fight back, or refuse to agree, you're accused of not having a sense of humour. They're the ones who don't have a sense of humour." This from a woman in a position of some responsibility, now in her early fifties.

Sexism in business is found not only in men and not only in humour. There are women, as there are men, who proclaim, almost with pride, that they do not like to work for women. Even some of those who deplore the attitude fall into the trap of generalizing. One of my correspondents, an accountant in a retail department store who by her other comments indicated her strong empathy with female colleagues, wrote: "Too many women still say, 'I don't like working for a woman.' *Every time this happens, they put down their own sex. This is the fault both of the worker and the woman in authority. A man when he gets a promotion nearly always expects it and takes it as his due; it doesn't change him much. Many of the gals get too competitive and try to drive their staff, instead of leading them. They often become nit-pickers and fault-finders and lose sight of the goal of doing a good job well – as a team*" (the emphasis is mine).

My correspondent has generalized from a small sampling. She has also, I believe, overlooked a fact of our culture: women – and men – will accept a man's driving and nit-picking, in fact may not even notice the characteristics because a man "is supposed to be the boss," to push and to criticize. The characteristics which are either not noticed or accepted without question in a man become objectionable in and to be avoided by a woman. Here I speak from my own experience and observation in my own profession. Too many times I have heard women school principals torn apart for trying to do what their male colleagues were doing with impunity and to applause.

The feeling, however, is there, no matter how much we may deplore it. "I employ only women," said Elsie, proprietor of a children's wear shop in a town of some twenty thousand people. "I find they work well together, are interested in their work, and are loyal to me. But you know something? Every time I get cornered by someone who asks me how I get women to work for me. They tell me women don't like to work for a woman boss. I don't know, I don't have that problem. I pay good wages; I give the girls time off when they need it, and their paid vacations. We're too small to have a pension scheme, not that I wouldn't want it. I can't afford it. But this business of women not liking to work for women! Honestly, we're no crazier to work for than some of the men I've had dealings with. Believe me!"

And men. Morris J. manages a candy and pastry shop for Honoré, who has three similar shops in an urban area. "You bet I get kidded about having two women bosses, one at home and one at work." He shrugged expressively. "Sure, Honoré can be a hellion. She's got a temper that goes off like a firecracker, and once or twice she has called me every name in the book and a few more when I didn't handle things just the way she would have. Funny. At first I thought I couldn't take that sort of thing from a woman. Then I remembered what I had taken from my previous employer. And I said to myself, 'I guess she has as much right to blow her top as any other boss. She's fair, when she cools down, and she is a darn good businesswoman. I've got a good job. I'm going places. I'll take Honoré just as she is.' "

John Johnston tells Morris he is a nut to take what he does from any woman. Johnston is an ex-Army type. He informed both Morris and me in no uncertain terms that no woman would ever push him around on the job because he would never take a job where the boss was a female, and that was that. There was a place for women and business was not it. "You mean," I asked him innocently, "all those office jobs and waitresses' jobs and sales clerks' jobs should be filled by men? There wouldn't be enough of you to go round."

"Come off it," he said disgustedly. "You know what I mean. I don't think women should be bosses to begin with, and it's okay for girls to work until they get married, or maybe some poor widows have to support themselves. The rest of them are better off at home looking after their husbands and families. We wouldn't have so many broken homes if women minded their own business instead of trying to run someone else's."

I have already discussed this kind of sexism as inhibiting women's movement into positions of responsibility and policy making in the business world. It is also a cause of petty annoyance and major frustration for those women who work in an environment where they are daily exposed to its enunciation in one form or another.

Closely related is the attitude of many people, men, women, family members, neighbours, to working mothers. The majority work because they must to support themselves and their children, if they are sole-support parents, or to supplement family incomes. In retrospect those whose children have now grown up believe that their children did not suffer as a result of the mothers' having worked, but they recall, sometimes with amusement, more often with sympathy for their younger selves, the agonies of guilt they suffered when they made the decision to leave home for work. "Even though I knew that I had no other choice I felt guilty, as if it were my fault that I had to work to support my children," Mina Klassen told me. "I worked in a small office, and I was often called to the telephone by name. For months every time that happened I was sure that something had happened to one of the kids, and my hand would be shaking when I picked up the phone. I never quite got over the feeling, though my eldest daughter used to get after me for being such a worry wart."

Mrs. Klassen's frustration came not from the real problem of lack of adequate care for her children but from the feeling of guilt that was projected on her by her own upbringing, by her neighbours, by her employer, "a fine man, who really cared about us girls who worked for him." He asked her regularly and anxiously how she was making out with the children, and did she worry about them when she was away all day? "He would have felt awful if he had known that he was really asking me whether it was right and proper for a mother of young children to work. He didn't think it was, but couldn't offer me an alternative! I know he believed that a mother's place is at home."

Single women and married women whose husbands are also working have a different kind of guilt thrust upon them, especially if they are in jobs that might be held by men. There are always some types, male and female, but most often women at home, who resent the working women

102

on the basis that they are depriving men with families of jobs. Times of high unemployment bring the resentment clearly out into the open and accentuate the guilt feelings that working women so easily acquire. The argument has been used to justify higher pay scales for men, cost-of-living bonuses based on sex, and the strong resistance to placing women in positions that pay well. The residue of the resentment and the feelings of guilt are still there.

One of the most common causes of frustration and annoyance to be brought to my attention was the requirement of women to do subservient tasks that were unrelated to the job for which they were hired. "Looking back I suppose I shouldn't have been so annoyed that I was asked to serve tea or coffee whenever my boss was having a conference. I was the secretary of the conference in every sense. I made the arrangements for it, took the notes, edited and prepared the minutes. Why should I be delegated to get the coffee? Even now when I am a company department manager – when someone else takes the minutes – I am sort of expected, as the only woman there, to do the honours with coffee. I resist. And I don't expect the secretary to do it either."

A beautifully prepared booklet called *let's pretend we work in the bank*[1] carrying the logo of the Royal Bank of Canada and aimed at children, is a perfect example of the stereotyping of male and female roles in the banks. On page 15 there is a colour photograph of a boy as the bank president dictating to a charming little girl acting the part of his secretary. On page 14, facing the photograph, under the heading "Secretary to the President," there appears the following verse:

"Take a letter, Miss Smith,
Then a memo or two.
And please phone our man in Japan when you're through.
Tell him I'm planning a trip in July.
Oh, and then call the airport –
Of course I shall fly."
"Sir, I've done all the filing, taken phone calls galore,
Typed so many letters my fingers are sore.
I've arranged a board meeting
Tomorrow at three
For all the directors.
May I get you some tea?"

On the last page, as an acknowledgement, the publisher made the statement: *"let's pretend we work in the bank* marks the debut of a series of books for children designed to develop knowledge and understanding of

Canadian business and industry. Psycan, on behalf of its young readers and the author, gratefully wishes to acknowledge the significance of the contribution of The Royal Bank of Canada to the development and production of this first in a series of *let's pretend* books." The booklet bears a 1973 copyright, and though I believe it is not now being circulated because of the furore it raised among women's organizations and the Advisory Council on the Status of Women, the very fact that it could as late as 1973 be sponsored with pride by the Royal Bank is proof that women's position in the business world is changing only slowly, slowly.

Said another secretary, "I don't really mind serving coffee – I have noticed that the so-called administrative assistants do the same, so maybe it is part of the job. I do resent being used as my boss's personal secretary. I get a good salary as women's salaries go, and I have a responsible position. The work I have to do is important. So why should my good and valuable time be used to pick up my boss's laundry, to buy a birth-day present for his fifteen-year-old son, and that sort of thing? I'm usually at the office after everyone else has gone in order to finish the legitimate work I have to do, so I do his errands on my own time, at lunch or after work. He wouldn't ask any of the men in the office to do these joe jobs. Look, I'm not crabbing about the ordinary courtesies. I mean, when we work through lunch I'll go out and pick up sandwiches, and I even type up his wife's club meeting minutes. I'm glad to be obliging. But I don't like being used as if I were a servant."

"As if I were a servant" and "I don't like being used." More and more independent women are voicing their feelings of resentment against doing tasks not related to the jobs for which they are paid, particularly when those tasks are personal services of the kind generally delegated to women.

A few of my correspondents complained of the dull, routine nature of their jobs. Women like Colleen, who were sole-support mothers, found themselves on a treadmill from which they could not escape because of their low qualifications and their desperate need for security; but on the whole, women, at least those with whom I spoke, have the capacity of finding interest in what they are doing. Indeed, I felt – and feel – some concern that so many women expressed such satisfaction with what they were doing, seemed to derive so much pleasure from it. Their content-ment pinpointed for me at least part of the problem to be solved by those who are dismayed by the low status of most women in business: low as manifested by poor pay, inadequate provision for old age and dependants, few opportunities for movement into positions of responsibility and policy making.

If so many women are so happy about their status, about the kinds of work they do, they are surely not too far removed from the house slaves who were contented with the limited favours and security their masters provided for them.

I do not want to be misunderstood. There is nothing wrong with being happy in the service. To be tied for one's working life to a job one hates must lead to madness. It's a fine thing to enjoy what one is doing. Besides, every job has its interesting elements; every job can go beyond the narrow limits set by the job description.

But from time to time, reading and listening, I began to wonder at our submissiveness as women, at our capacity to accept what was essentially work beneath our ability and to make the best of it.

"I learned to enjoy my work – whatever," wrote a Saskatoon accountant.

"A cardinal rule I have followed all my life is to look for things to enjoy in any job I had to do," a buyer in the fashion department of a large department store said to me.

"Maybe I am crazy but I like what I am doing. You might find it dull and routine and repetitive, but I like it because it is orderly. I enjoy having things come out even. I know I am doing a good job, too," said a young woman who spends eight hours a day working at a machine.

"I do the kind of work I can do well," a middle-aged woman wrote to me. "My life was empty. Not that I don't love my husband and my family and my home. They come first with me. But when I realized that I was looking forward to the Thursday afternoon bridge game with 'the girls' as a high point of the week I decided it was time for me to get out. I took a refresher course to bring up my typing and shorthand, and I am working – have been for about three years. I am a university graduate; I worked for five years before I was married, but that was a long time ago, and right now there is not much I can do except the routine work I am doing. I don't care. I love it. I am seeing people again, people who know me as me, and not because I have a house, or kids, or a husband. So it's routine but not as routine as dusting and putting away the laundry and playing bridge every Thursday afternoon. At least I am doing it with people around, different people. When I come back to the dusting and putting away the laundry I can bear it because I also have something else. Yes, my work is satisfying. Anyway for now."

The list of satisfactions was far longer than the list of frustrations. Most of the satisfaction expressed centred on the pleasure derived from doing things for people, from being of service, from helping others to achieve, thereby confirming the findings of formal and informal studies of the subject. From all parts of Canada and from women in various kinds of jobs the word comes loud and clear:

- British Columbia, from a woman engaged in the marketing and public relations aspects of banking: "My present work is satisfying because I feel confident that I am providing a worthwhile training to other employees and that I am giving the bank's customers the best service possible. I enjoy the encounters with people."
- Edmonton, from Anne Stimpson, owner and operator of a school for receptionists: "My work is *very* satisfying . . . helping people find a better way of life through teaching them personal worth, and living up to their potential."
- Regina, from a life insurance agent: "I enjoy helping people. I am doing something to guarantee their future security."
- Winnipeg, from a real estate salesperson: "Very satisfying. As well as making a lot of money there is the satisfaction of making people happy by finding them what they want."
- Yellowknife, from the owner of a ladies' ready-to-wear store: "I love my work and like to be successful and make people satisfied."
- Quebec City, from a bank teller: "I work with many people and enjoy serving them."
- Fredericton, from a young woman in a small shop: "I like my work because I am helping people make good choices."

Some women, like the middle-aged woman who had had enough of her Thursday bridge games, find their jobs satisfying for intensely personal reasons:

- "My job makes me feel a person, respected for what I am and do, and not because I am my children's mother, my husband's wife. . . ."
- "To me my job is my life. I am part of it and it is part of me. It is a sort of fulfilment. Does that sound silly? My work is creative, and I grow with it." (This came from a woman who is in industrial design.)
- "I realize now that I have learned a lot and have been able to improve myself by being in the business world," was Zetta's comment.

One aspect of self-fulfilment is to receive recognition for what one is doing; that ranks high as a reason for job satisfaction.

- Evelyn MacLachlan wrote: "I have a great feeling of satisfaction in working on a building, bridge, dam, etc., especially if it is a prestige job that is in the news and everyone knows about it."
- Anne Shepherd of Medicine Hat wrote: "It is good to receive compliments on the work [I do], often from the most unlikely quarters."
- A stenographer in Halifax said, "The man I work for is terrific. He tells me when I do something right, or come up with a good idea. It gives me a good feeling to know that what I do is appreciated."
- "My work is absolutely satisfying. One looks nice and feels nice because one has entrée into another world. It gives one a sense of participating in a bit of the action, and makes one feel more alive. . . . People express admiration for your attempt and are ready with encouragement . . . great ego trips!" That is how Alma Lorelei Meis sees her work.

Making money is another important element of job satisfaction. "My job pays well, and I can live nicely on what I make. I can't complain about it," is the essence of what many people have to say about their work.

"I can put up with quite a bit for the good salary I am earning," an acquaintance told me. "You may not think that is a good reason for being satisfied with my job, but I think it is. For many years I worked for a bare living wage."

"Other people may tell you that they work for the love of working. Don't believe them," a sceptical young woman said to me. "They like the money they are earning and what it can buy for them. It gives me a sense of independence that *I* love, and I am willing to put in long hours and accept a lot of extra responsibility for that pay cheque every two weeks. Of course I like what the job entails as well. . . . I work with people, but the frustrations might outweigh the satisfactions if the pay were not quite as good as it is."

And another woman who asked to remain anonymous said candidly, "I stick to the job I'm in because I need the money. It's the only honest satisfaction I get out of it, and if I could afford to quit I would leave with a day's notice."

The middle-aged bridge player enjoyed her job because it took her out of her home. She was not alone in giving this as a reason for job satisfaction. Variety appeals to women, as it must to men as well, and work outside the home provides that variety – and money into the bargain.

A retail clerk in Saint John, New Brunswick, finds her job interesting because it gets her away from home for a few hours several times a week. She enjoys the excitement of sales and seeing and talking to so many people. A cashier in a northern Saskatchewan city works evenings and loves her work because it "gets me away from home, lets me do something useful *for money* [the italics are hers], and gives my husband a taste of what it means to cope with the kids for a few hours at a time. It's good for both of us."

A Burnaby filing clerk likes the orderliness of her job. She doesn't find it tedious. She works in a congenial office and has met some interesting people she would never have met at home. The money she earns has made it possible to buy much-needed furniture and to set aside something for a long-hoped-for visit to the Old Country to see her parents; she is an only daughter and they are not getting any younger.

Flexibility of hours is important to women with home responsibilities. Women who are selling encyclopaedias or real estate or insurance almost all gave freedom from set times as one of the reasons for doing the type of work they had selected for themselves.

Jean MacDonald, the Westmount real estate agent, says, "I enjoy my work as it gives me the chance to establish my own hours and make as much money as I need. Being a little (not wildly) successful has had its monetary satisfactions, but best of all I have had ample time to spend with my son. Being in a one-parent situation I have found it absolutely necessary to have two or more hours free each day to be with my child."

A self-employed woman from Toronto, happily married, said: "I love the job I am doing now. It's creative, satisfying, and I have only myself to account to. I can work when I like, as long as I like, and the responsibilities are mine as well as the goals and aims I set myself. I can either succeed at it or fail at it. I guess I like the freedom from restrictions."

As so many women indicated, they find their jobs satisfying for a complex of reasons. Not the least of them, of course, is the nature of the job itself, as several of the quotations in this chapter clearly show.

A division manager in a Hamilton retail store wrote: "My work is satisfying because of the responsibility involved. (I do the buying for my department, set up display plans, hire full-time help, etc.) There is constant variety, independence . . . and I work with such good people."

An accountant, also in a retail store, this time in Saskatoon, wrote: "I have always found the work I have had to do a challenge and have had great satisfaction in meeting the challenge. My work has almost always been varied enough that there's never a dull moment, and often the days are not long enough and I'm surprised when they come to an end. Analysing statistics, balancing, planning, and solving problems give me a terrific lift. Helping my staff meet their deadlines, working with them, helping to train them to become more efficient is a wonderful feeling. They are the greatest; when we come through in the clinches we all get a lift – and they know I am proud of them and appreciate them."

The executive secretary to the director of a Montreal CEGEP said, "I find that my work is very satisfying in that I get to be involved and know about the decisions being made in our organization. My boss knows that I am trustworthy and can treat information confidentially. I appreciate the trust and the respect I receive."

Few satisfactions are as great as doing a job well and seeing it through to its completion, as Helen Young, the systems representative, testifies. There is a feeling of accomplishment "in following the steps: ascertaining how a prospective customer is handling the accounting function being considered and outlining a system which will save the customer time and money; designing a special system to meet special needs of the customer when the standard system cannot be used; providing the Toronto plant with design specifications for printing; installing the system in the customer's office; making a call-back contact to find out if the system is working as anticipated. The cycle of sales involvement brings satisfaction when it is completed satisfactorily, when the system proves to be adequate, and when the customer is entirely satisfied." Ms. Young adds that there is also satisfaction in "meeting and surpassing monthly and yearly company quotas, and in the monetary increase as sales performance improves," the tangible proofs of success.

A survey conducted by the Women's Bureau in Manitoba in 1974 showed women as less concerned about the monetary rewards than about the value of the work they were doing.[2] Again, though the philosophy behind the concern is admirable, I must wonder whether the attitudes it reveals are not part of the cultural conditioning of women. Women in our society are tacitly expected to serve without reward other than the approval of those whom they love or respect. The whole structure of volunteerism is built on the premise that women should work without being paid, as is the general, if lessening, belief that household work should not be paid for, that the wife and mother works for the joy of serving her loved ones, for her keep and spending money.

The acceptance of this philosophy has contributed to the low economic status of women. It has also helped to inhibit the organization for the purpose of bargaining of many occupational groups in which women predominate. It was good, therefore, to note how many women admitted without a feeling of guilt that a major cause of satisfaction with their work was that the monetary returns were good.

"Women don't want to undertake responsibility." How many times I have heard that statement made; and yet among the women I talked with a great many told me that their work was frustrating because it entailed little responsibility, and many more told me how satisfying their work was because it carried responsibility and involved decision making.

In the book *Women in Canada*, Meredith M. Kimball wrote on "Women and Success: A Basic Conflict." The article reports on a study carried on in Vancouver schools at the Grade 8 and Grade 12 levels, and it reinforces what most of us who have had dealings with girls and young women of fourteen and eighteen could have told the researchers on the basis of our experience. The study suggested that in high school and college women are most fearful of success when they have to make the most important decisions of their lives. The writer says, "It seems that it is not so much that women see no value in successful achievement, but rather that they see successful achievement as conflict-provoking, precisely because success is both desired and threatening. . . . One can generally expect that most competitive achievement situations will be anxiety-provoking to women."[3]

Kimball's study, incidentally, also pointed to what might be a lessening of the competitive drive among boys as well as girls, or perhaps a similar "fear of success." The experimenters were surprised to find how many students, more than half of both the girls and the boys surveyed, consistently chose the moderately successful person over the highly successful person as the happier of the two.

It was remarkable to me, too, how many of the women who wrote or spoke to me were content with what they were doing, had little ambition to try anything else, in fact, felt defensive at any suggestion that they might be successful at a higher level of responsibility or in a job that had higher risk but paid better. More than once I was reminded by a woman that she was not going to fall victim to the Peter principle.

A successful woman, president of a personnel placement firm in British Columbia, wrote: "In my involvement in the personnel placement field I find that management is encouraging women – women are afraid to succeed – it is unfeminine – it might jeopardize their marital security."

Students in business education and younger girls who had not yet made their choice were often frank in admitting to me that they did not want to be (or to appear to be) smarter than the boys in the class.

Repeatedly I have seen excellent students, girls who had consistently topped their classes until they were fourteen or fifteen, deliberately, I am sure, slough their studies when they wanted to attract or hold a boy who was not a good student. Success in their studies constituted a threat; their achievement was, in Kimball's terms, conflict-provoking, because it was both desired and threatening.

How threatening achievement can be was demonstrated by the women who told me that their marriages had broken under the strain of their business success, and by those other women who believe that if they are to become successful in their business careers they must remain unmarried. It is sad that both men and women should contribute to the threat by their acceptance of the belief that a woman's success must undermine a man's ego. Yet for every woman who blamed the break-up of her marriage on her success, there was a woman who gave her husband and her family credit for making her success possible. Over the past few years I have listened to men who were deeply hurt at the "chauvinist" insults hurled at them.

"My wife and I have shared all the work of our home from the day we were married," an indignant husband and father protested to an accusing young woman. "We both work; we both contribute to the family pot; we both have money of our own; and we truly share our lives. What makes me so damn mad is your unjustified generalization. I am not unique. I don't expect to be patted on the head for doing what seems to me and to my wife and to all our friends to be the natural thing. Our sons and daughter see us sharing the household work, and young as they are they pitch in too. There's no women's work or men's work, boys' work or girls' work in our house."

"Okay, okay," his antagonist conceded, "so you share the household chores. But tell me honestly. What would happen if your wife's firm decided that she should be transferred, say, to Halifax? Or if she got an offer from another company at a fantastic salary provided she moved to another city? Would you throw up your good job to go along?"

"So far we haven't faced that choice," the indignant husband said to her, "but if we had to we would solve the problem as we have met other major crises in the family. We would sit down, all of us, my wife, the children and I, and weigh the pros and cons, decide what it would do to the family as a whole if we decided one way or the other, maybe canvass possibilities of my company moving me. I can't tell you how we would resolve the matter. The answer would depend on what was best for all of us. It certainly wouldn't be decided on the basis of my wife not being able to move because my job always comes first."

I don't think the accusing young woman believed him. I did.

In any event the successful women among my sampling enjoyed their success. Whatever conflicts they may have had initially seem to have been resolved once they found that success brought with it rewards of self-esteem and self-confidence, that the pleasures of achievement did not always or necessarily diminish their attractiveness to men or their attachment to their families.

Helen Young, however, added a word of caution: "As more women move into positions of influence they may become heir to physical problems associated with the pressures of business – ulcers, heart attacks, etc. If so, they may have reason to question the benefit of being in the upper echelons of the command of business."

She may be right. On the other hand, I remember a noted psychiatrist from whom I took classes in mental health many years ago quoting statistics which have since been corroborated by other, later studies. It seems that there is a much lesser incidence of mental ill health among women working outside the home than among homemakers in their middle years, and – a necessary concomitant – such women suffered less from minor physical ailments and were generally more contented.

In any event, if my sampling is any indicator, women at work find fewer frustrations than satisfactions in their employment and are happiest when the work they do carries some responsibility, especially when it is recognized through appreciation and adequate pay. They dislike and frequently resent sex-based humour, not because they are prudish or lack the ability to laugh at themselves but because they find it demeaning and humiliating. They enjoy work they believe has human value and contributes to the well-being of those with and for whom they work. Conversely, some of them feel that they are being used and that their work and their ability are being undervalued, especially when they are required to do service chores that are unrelated to the job they are paid to do.

Fear of success accounts in part for the unwillingness of some women to undertake positions of responsibility, a fear that stems perhaps from the mistaken belief – or feeling – that woman's success automatically undermines man's ego. Even when men assure young women that this is not necessarily the case the women are sceptical. Old, deeply engrained cultural patterns are hard to alter. Besides, there is comfort in the feeling that if I don't try I cannot fail and the illusion that if I had really wanted to try I could have succeeded. Better the comfortable feeling and the illusion than the risk.

What qualities should a woman have if she wants to succeed in business? What qualifications should she have to succeed?

6

Having What It Takes

I was sitting across an impressive desk in an impressive office as I asked these questions of a woman – I'll call her Ms. Miller – whose surroundings proclaimed her to be successful, and I got the answer I deserved. "If I may be so rude," she said to me, "these are silly questions, poorly defined and therefore difficult to answer. In the first place, may I ask what you mean by 'business'? And what exactly do you mean by 'succeeding'? When you answer my questions, maybe I can apply some intelligence to the answering of yours."

I explained that I was limiting my definition of business to what might be called finance, trade, and commerce, and that I was listening to women engaged at various levels in those arenas, some working for others, some self-employed.

"Good," she said. "That covers my first question. Now what about the second one? What do you mean by 'success'? To my way of thinking there are all kinds of success. Mrs. Smith, who showed you in just now, is to my way of thinking a success. She is doing well what she enjoys doing. She must be about the same age as I am and she'll never make the top of the heap, if you define success in terms of prestige, high salary, or what have you. But she's a successful businesswoman because the job she is doing here is well done. She is appreciated by me, and I tell her so. She is making enough money to keep her in relative comfort and is, I think, a happy person. So she's successful. The qualities she needs to make her successful aren't really all that different from those needed by the little girl you see out there at the filing cabinet, although in some ways Mrs. Smith has a lot more responsibility. Who knows? Maybe the little file clerk will be sitting at my desk one day if she has the qualities Mrs. Smith isn't showing right now, the drive and ambition a woman needs when she decides that she is going to compete in a man's world. At this moment in time she is content to be successful in what is essentially a woman's world – the outside office. Or she is more interested in another kind of business – catching that young fellow she's been making eyes at ever since she came here. No, I'm being snide now, and I don't like myself when I make that kind of glib remark. That girl is careful about her work; she rarely makes a mistake, and she's smart enough to

113

ask when she doesn't know something. I'd say that in today's changing world she has a better chance than I had of making it. And I managed, so why shouldn't she? Even if she gets her man along the way."

Ms. Miller walked over to the window, and waved to me to join her. "Look down there," she said, "across the street. That department store employs hundreds of women, thousands if you count its other branches. How many of them have the qualities to get them into the board room?"

She interrupted herself with a laugh and went on, "Not that having the qualities would help a woman to make the board room of that outfit. Unless she were born with a gold spoon in her mouth or maybe management thought it would boost sales radically to have a token female on the board.

"Anyway, to get back to my point. Would you honestly say that all the women working in minor jobs in that store are unsuccessful in business just because they are not executives of the company or managers of departments? I wouldn't. I buy all my clothes – well, almost all my clothes – in that store. The woman who looks after me is a very successful saleswoman. She knows me and what I like and need. She has regular customers who won't buy from anyone but her. She likes her work. She has turned down a better job – that is, one with more responsibility and more money – because she didn't want the headaches that went with it. I call her a successful businesswoman."

Would Ms. Miller, I asked, have felt successful if she had spent twenty years in the same job, no matter how interesting it might have been initially? She corrected me immediately. "No job is the same for twenty years. If my saleswoman over there hadn't grown with her job she wouldn't be as good as she is now. She needed qualities that I hope I have to be as successful as she is. Flexibility is one of them, the ability to change with changing conditions, with changing clientele, with changing environment. She merely made a different choice than I did because of her different definition of personal success, or success in business, if you like. Anyway, the point I am trying to make is that success does have different definitions and we are too quick to think of it in hierarchical terms."

"And in financial terms?" I asked.

"You probably won't believe me," she said with considerable feeling, "but at this stage in my life – I am forty-eight – the money means less to me than the game itself. I enjoy business, the give and the take, the challenge of something new every day, every week. I suppose I even enjoy the stresses and the strains. Yes, the money is important, and I make sure that I earn as much as the men in similar positions; but it is important at this stage more as a symbol of what I am able to do – you know, like the crest on a kid's jacket to show he's made the winning team – than for spending. I could have stopped long ago. I'm busy. I can spend only so much, and you know what happens to savings these days. But I make no bones about it. I like being competitive. I like being successful. Maybe when I tell you these things I am telling you what qualities I think a successful businesswoman should have. At least one who measures success for herelf as I do, not as Mrs. Smith does or my saleswoman across the street."

Ms. Miller supported what has already been said in the previous chapter about women's ambivalence towards success. She is well aware of the conflicts that wrack women as they enter work arenas where they have to compete for place, especially with men.

She also made abundantly clear to me how easily I had fallen into the trap of defining success in terms of position in the hierarchy. Success, like love, is a many-splendoured thing. The woman who works part time as a check-out clerk in a supermarket is in her way as successful as Ms. Miller.

Obviously, then, the qualities required for success are related to the kind of success and the kind of job in which it is achieved. Unquestioning willingness to follow an order, for example, could conceivably make for success in what M. P. Marchak calls jobs with low-level job control,[1] whereas the same quality militates against the success of women in jobs where they are expected to question and to think at any level of responsibility. Nothing is more annoying, time consuming, and therefore costly and inefficient than having to correct the work of a clerk or typist who has unthinkingly and unquestioningly copied a minor error in transcription or dictation.

Reva Lander of Vancouver, who describes herself as "consultant – word processing and support services," pointed out that the type of business also helps to determine the qualities required for success. The Quebec woman who runs a successful commercial art gallery and the woman in Edmonton who is in the business of commercial design both believe that an important part of their success comes from their creativity, from the fact that essentially they are and think of themselves as artists first and businesswomen second. Nor were they the only women who mentioned creativity as an integral and integrating factor in their success. The florist, the owner of a "fashion shop," the industrial engineer, the systems analyst, the president of the Bakery Council of

Canada would probably all agree that creativity is important to their success. On the other hand, not one of the accountants, the bank managers, the insurance representatives used the word either in describing the satisfaction they felt in their work or the qualities required to succeed in it. So though primary business skills and management skills may not differ very much from one type of business to another, the qualities for success in different kinds of business may differ substantially. The woman who makes a success of a commercial art gallery may be as ruthless or as sensitive as the woman who successfully operates a hardware store, but she – if no one else – believes that she needs the additional qualities of creativity and empathy with artists. The woman hardware dealer does not need or feel the same empathy for her wholesaler or the manufacturer of her products.

I was reminded by Ms. Miller and others that the qualities making for success are not necessarily different for men and women, especially if success is defined in terms of movement up through the ranks of the hierarchy rather than in terms of personal contentment or giving satisfaction to an employer. They remarked that I should be asking not so much about qualities required for success as about qualities women should have in a greater or less degree than men competing for the same types of work or the same rung on the ladder.

Like courage, Reva Lander noted. Moyra Roberts agreed when she said that a woman "needs guts – more guts, and possibly a sugar daddy." And she added, "So does a man."

Women need more courage and a different kind of courage because of the unspoken prejudice they face, the hostility that amounts almost to paranoia, I was told by a woman who owns and operates her own business (hardware and building supplies). "Let's face it," she said. "If there is only so much room at the top someone gets pushed out when more people scramble for the summit. If three women were to be added to three men now clawing their way up and even one of the women makes it to the top, one of the men is going to be left out. You really have to have guts to face that kind of fighting. Not very many of us have been trained for it, and we chicken out long before we get anywhere near the top."

Others expressed the same thought less forcefully. "A woman needs to be twice as good in her field as any man in the same line of work. She surely needs a stubborn streak as otherwise she could be persuaded to give up," one of my correspondents wrote. "Too many men are more likely to say, very often with genuine concern, 'You don't want that sort

116

of job; it is too strenuous [disturbing, demanding]' to a woman than to another man."

Stubbornness in this sense is not far removed from a quality mentioned again and again – stick-to-it-iveness, the ability to complete a task, not to give up, if it is something that must be done, merely because it becomes difficult or unpleasant. "Funny thing about some of us women who have been looked after most of our lives," an ambitious middle-aged woman said to me. "We sort of automatically expect at first that someone else will do the dirty work, and when the heat is on, we fold. I learned the hard way by losing my first job after I was divorced. I needed the job, and not only for the money, but I had a tendency to throw up my hands and say 'I can't' when I was given something tough to do."

It takes courage to stick to something that is tough, and "strength, endurance, and confidence," to quote Reva Lander again.

Confidence in this context means self-confidence. It ranks high as a quality needed for success and low among qualities most working women possess.

- "You have to know that you can do what you are undertaking and must convince other people that you can do it."
- "You have to be quietly confident in your own ability without being brash about it. In that way you inspire confidence in other people who work with you and whom you approach in the line of your business."
- "Women tend to deprecate their own ability. Being overly modest doesn't get you anywhere. Instead it makes other people uncomfortable when they have to reassure you that you are okay. Don't be afraid to say that you can do something. But be sure that you can."

A Charlottetown stenographer rates high the ability to rise above personalities, something that women are supposed to have in smaller quantity than men. "Why is it," a male employer complained, "that when I make a general statement about something every woman in the place takes it personally and is sure I am talking about her?"

Nariman K. Dhalla, writing in a book called *These Canadians, A Sourcebook of Marketing and Socio-economic Facts* – facts, if you please! – accepts the characteristic as peculiarly feminine: "Perhaps the most prominent feminine characteristic is the tendency to personalize. A man *by nature* [the italics are mine] follows an objective line of reasoning. A woman, by contrast, is inclined to look at each person, each product, each idea, each remark personally and emotionally. Her

117

thinking is largely subjective. She translates everything into personal terms. A theoretical discussion, for example, on the regulation of international trade may soon disintegrate into an argument about the family budget."

It may be feminine of me to remark that international trade might be conducted on a more reasonable basis if those engaging in it bore in mind its effects on the family budget. In any event the complaints reminded me of a story I read years ago. A speaker was delivering a lecture to a group of suffragettes on the topic of – what else? – Women.

"I admire you ladies," he said, "I admire your stamina, your devotion to duty, your ability to make us men do exactly what you want. You have only one weakness. You can't generalize. When a general statement is made, you immediately apply it to yourself."

At this point a stout woman in the front row leaped to her feet and shouted indignantly, "*I* don't."

Unfair, unfair. If I may be permitted to generalize, the frailty is a human one shared by both sexes.

Nevertheless the ability to accept criticism, to fight for a principle without becoming emotional, to maintain a businesslike approach was cited repeatedly as an element required for success. "Men seem to be able to react to criticism and argue against it, make a case against it, more successfully than women," one of my correspondents wrote. "I've often wondered why, and I've come to the conclusion that there are at least two reasons. One is that it is expected for men to become angry; it is not ungentlemanly or unmanly, whereas it is unladylike for a woman to blow her top. She becomes a virago or a shrew or something equally disagreeable. A second reason is that men get red in the face but their eyes don't fill with tears when they are angry. When I get mad, my eyes fill and overflow. It is NOT a sign of weakness but of righteous indignation, but the men take it as weakness."

My correspondent referred to unfair criticism. Other women believed it important to be able to accept and benefit from deserved criticism.

Diplomacy! Women have to be more diplomatic than men. Women must give criticism more carefully than men if it is to be accepted by either men or women. Women cannot say some things to their colleagues, customers, or the people who work under them that men in a similar situation could say with impunity. "It's a good thing so many of us have been trained from childhood to get our own way indirectly," a middle management woman said, to be set upon quickly and vociferously by others in our small discussion group.

"That's the trouble with so many of us," one young woman stated firmly. "We don't play fair. Diplomacy I agree with, but manipulation and using feminine wiles, whatever they are, go against my grain. If that's the way we operate, I can't blame the men who don't think we are ready for responsibility."

"Come on, now. That's not what she meant. She's just saying that there's more than one way to skin a cat, and there's no use antagonizing people when you can get around them. *I* think that's something a lot of men can learn from us." This from a woman in her middle thirties who had said very little during an hour's discussion.

"Diplomacy, yes. But an open kind of diplomacy, please. Being sensitive to people's feelings, that's good. Taking advantage of being a woman – that's bad," from a younger woman.

I wonder how she would have reacted to what a British Columbia politician, a woman of wide experience, cited as important qualities – "guile and a thorough knowledge of guerilla warfare."

Women, both successful and unsuccessful by their own evaluation, believe that influence and chance play significant roles in promoting success. Someone wrote, "It helps to have a rich father, husband, or friend."

- "I don't think I would ever have been able to raise the money to go into business for myself if some of my husband's (male) friends hadn't vouched for me."

- "The job I got was a token job, I know, because I happened to know the right people. I don't suppose anyone thought I would make anything big out of it."

- "You ask what qualities a woman needs to succeed. The most important is luck, just sheer luck."

- "For women particularly a lot depends on working for the right man at the right time, and that is often a matter of pure luck. When your boss moves up, you move up with him if you are any good at all. You can be just as good and get nowhere if your boss is not in line for promotion."

- "I suppose I could say that I was lucky and benefited from someone else's hard luck. My immediate superior had a severe heart attack. He was on sick leave and I carried on without him. Eventually he died, and the powers that be just 'forgot' to move anyone into his place. Why should they? I was doing the work for about one third of the money. Finally it occurred to dumb little me that I should have the title and the salary. I asked for it and got the first but not the second. Yeah, I did get a raise so I was making half of what he had got."

Influence, or chance, however, can at best be only the introduction to a job or a promotion. It is what women make of the job or the promotion that contributes to their success or immobility or failure. And for success women need the same qualities that men need; as Levine Moore of Saskatoon says, "all the virtues or a reasonable facsimile." But they need these virtues in greater strength and concentration, and in many instances they find that they have to overcome initial prejudice against their having the virtues.

How much femininity or femaleness or being a lady makes for success in business is a controversial subject. Some women see themselves limited by their femaleness, so that they say, "I believe we are biologically unfitted for the stresses of certain kinds of work, and we should stay out of them." And, "Our major responsibility to our children makes it impossible for us to think in terms of a career. We start too late."

Then there are the women who see femaleness as an advantage as was indicated in Chapter 4. They see no reason why they should not make use, as one woman said, "of the male image of me as a sex object." She would agree with the British Columbia politician that guile and guerilla warfare are legitimate strategies, and if her big blue eyes and 36-26-40 measurements disarm her opponent – well, why not?

On the other hand, another group feels that "a woman should never take advantage of her gender." That's not to say that charm and a warm personality are not important ingredients for success in almost any line of work; and a womanly personality is, as one charming young woman told me in all seriousness, inevitably different from a manly personality. But deliberately to use sex as a weapon, or even as a tool, is unethical and ultimately self-defeating. "It may be true," she said, "that in my work – I sell insurance – I am selling myself as well as my wares. That's what the first sales manual I was ever given said I should be doing. (Not in insurance, no. I was doing door-to-door selling then.) But anyway, whatever I sell, the product has to be worth a repeat order; it has to stand up. If I have sold it only on the basis of my personal charm, I'm a goner."

"However you look at it," another woman in the same field said, "we are in a highly competitive business. What's important is not how long

120

our eyelashes are, or whether we have good legs – except to carry us on our strenuous rounds – but our business ability, our shrewdness in knowing how much a prospect can afford to buy, our sensitivity in knowing how much protection he or she needs, our intelligence in being able to present a better case for our company's offerings than our competitor's. My experience as a woman who has benefited from insurance coverage, and my understanding of family problems have both been useful to me in my work; but no more useful than a man's experience may be along slightly different lines. I'm good at what I am doing because I believe in it and because I am willing to expend time and energy to make a success of it. I'd be ashamed to take advantage of my being a woman – even if it were to do me some good. I don't think it would."

This woman mentioned intelligence as an important attribute of success. Another added, "And executive ability." Intelligence and executive ability are not entirely god-given. Both can be cultivated. "Ask questions," I was told. "Don't be afraid to admit that you don't know something. What's bad is to have to ask the same question four or five times. Your knowledge and your ability to apply that knowledge fruitfully will develop if you keep your mind open and your thinking flexible. Knowing more about your job automatically makes your handling of it more intelligent; and it gives you opportunities to do things that bring your intelligence out in the open where it will be noticed. Watch how good executives operate, how they use their time, how they deal with people. You can learn a lot from them."

Intelligence and energy. Physical and mental energy is mentioned again and again by employers, particularly as an indicator of future success. "I can't stand dawdlers," a woman employer said impatiently. "The girl who takes ten minutes to get herself organized every time she sits down at her desk doesn't last very long with me. I tell her once, try to lay out a pattern for her, and if she doesn't smarten up I won't have her around. She's wasting my time, not hers."

"The girl who moves down the hall slowly and gracefully may make her fortune modelling. In our business she's a debit item. I can remember one who thought she was a Miss Canada candidate. Every time I came along behind her I wanted to give her a shove, preferably with my boot. My boss felt the same way, and she was eased out within a few months. Unfair? No, not at all. She was just too slow. We couldn't afford her." This comment was made by a woman who is now her own boss.

Employers were asked what they thought women needed to succeed in business. Some of the answers were short and to the point:

- "A woman should know what she is expected to do and do it with a minimum of fuss."
- "Qualities needed for success? No different than what I would expect a man to have if he wants to get on in the world."
- "They should ask no special favours or consideration. Women seem to want the best of both worlds: to be liberated and to be treated as the weaker sex."
- "Men don't like to be bossed, especially by a woman. The successful woman is the one who can convince a man that he is the boss, while she gets what she wants."
- "Looks and age are not important; good grooming and a pleasant personality are."

These remarks were all made by men who employ women.

Many of the suggestions were negative in form and were remarkably similar in tone whether they came from men or women employers. Some of the *don'ts* that I heard frequently were:

DON'T
> wear sexy clothes to work. It's embarrassing and distracting for men working with you.
> be bossy.
> manipulate, that is, try to run the boss and the office in underhand ways.
> be coy.
> try to be one of the boys.
> get emotional about criticism and take a general comment personally.
> expect special favours because you are a woman.
> wait to be asked if you want a promotion or to move to another kind of job in your company.

A friend of mine, a lawyer, answered my question at some length. "Women executives I know have several things in common. They all have an extraordinary amount of energy. They are all self-motivating and self-activating. I have noticed that they all have good memories, or at least make a point of remembering a good deal about a great many people. They look nice. I don't mean that they are good-looking, or beautiful, or even pretty. On the contrary, they are like the rest of us, everything from ordinary to downright homely, but they have an air about them that makes them look attractive. Above all, they know what they are talking about when they talk business, and they are usually well informed about a great many other things as well. In fact, they have all the qualities that a successful male executive should have. I must admit, though, that they do have something extra. They're female, and that can be very pleasant, too."

"You ask me what qualities a woman needs to be successful in business," said the manager of a company that employs women in its office and its plant. "It depends on the business, of course. If you are talking about a girl working in the office, I'll give you one list; if you are asking me about a woman who claws her way up to top management I'll give you another. And if you mean women in business for themselves there's a third set. In the office I want someone who is intelligent, but not so intelligent that she thinks she can tell me what to do. She should be able to spell, write a reasonable sentence, find out what I want to say and put it into readable English. She should be able to meet the public, pleasantly. I don't want her chewing gum in the office, holding private telephone conversations on the business phone, taking half-hour coffee breaks, having hysterics because her boy friend has ditched her. I think you get the picture. Oh, yes, I should have mentioned that I like her to dress conservatively, nicely but conservatively. None of this no-bra nonsense at work."

Chris is a young man whose ability and background have helped him move quickly to the top in the business of his choice. He is married to a woman who is a practising lawyer. They have two children. "The ambitious woman – yes. I work with some excellent people who happen to be women. Our relationship is strictly business. We respect one another just as we respect colleagues of the same sex. Let's see. The qualities that I think make them successful. I suppose the same as those that make anyone successful. They have lots of drive, lots of ambition, and a hell of a lot of self-confidence. At least they give that impression. My wife tells me that their self-confidence is as shaky as mine sometimes is. They know their business; they work hard at it. Maybe they tend to be more touchy than we men are, and maybe they have a right to be. One of the gals practically blows her top when anyone makes a joke about women's liberation. I can't say I blame her. I'm getting sick of the subject myself."

Richard L. is in the food-processing business. "I've never worked *for* a woman though I have worked with a lot of women, so I can't say whether women are harder or easier to work for than men, but I know that women have to be a damn sight more careful about what they say and do than any man in the same position. I hear some of the bitching that goes on about a woman who I happen to think is tops in her field, and who is no harder on the people who work for her than I am, for example. Diplomacy, that's what a woman needs in business. She has to be diplomatic, more diplomatic than most men have to be. Maybe that's changing. I'm not sure."

The male owner of a women's dress shop in a small city knows many women in the same position as he is. Before he branched out for himself he was a department manager in a large urban chain store. About self-employed women he had this to say: "Well, it's a miserable, competitive world we live in. Women and men both have to fight, have to be ruthless to make it to the top, or even halfway there. I know quite a number of women who have done reasonably well in small businesses, and very few who have made it in a big way. But the odds are against them. I'd guess there would be more of them if the atmosphere were better. Look how well they do in middle management. Besides, I have a feeling that a lot of you gals don't really want to make it big. The price is too high. You may be right. But the fact remains, if you want to make it you have to be able to fight, to take the gaff."

And inevitably there is the character who says, in a manner that makes it possible for him to laugh it off as a joke if you protest: "If you ask me, and you have asked, the only successful businesswoman is the kid who gets into a field where there are lots of eligible men, finds herself a husband, and settles down to what God made her to do – look after a husband and kids. Come on now. You know as well as I do why girls go into Commerce and Business Admin. They're not interested in a degree, just a certificate. A marriage certificate. They don't need any special qualities or qualifications for that. They're born with them. Heh, heh, heh."

All right, so a woman is intelligent, creative, diplomatic, in short has most of the qualities her peers and her competitors consider necessary for success in business. Sometimes she becomes successful, sometimes she does not. Or a woman has some of the qualities and characteristics that make for success, but lacks competitiveness, aggressiveness, drive, ambition – that single most important ingredient that starts her on her way and keeps her moving.

According to those sociologists and psychologists who have studied the ingredients of success in women, specifically in businesswomen, two factors are of paramount importance: the family into which a girl is

124

born and her position in the family. In 1968 Margaret M. Hennig made an in-depth study of twenty-five of the one hundred female presidents or vice-presidents of medium-to-large nationally recognized business firms in the United States; at that time there were no more than one hundred, so her sample was a large one.[2] The similarities among the backgrounds of these women were astounding.

Every one of the twenty-five was either an only child or the first child in a family of no more than three girls; that is, in all cases the families were all-girl. There were no brothers.

All were born into middle-class families living on or near the eastern seaboard of the United States.

The parents of all of them had at least completed high school.

All the women reported close family relationships, with respect, support, and high expectations from both parents.

Both parents valued in the women during their childhood femaleness and achievement, activity and competitive success.

The girls who grew up to be successful businesswomen, then, were because of their upbringing – and their upbringing was related in some degree to their position in the family, and to the kind of family in which they were brought up – spared the conflict so many women suffer from between achievement and femininity, a conflict that came through clearly in the comments of many of my correspondents. Achievement, as so many of them noted, is closely related to self-confidence and self-esteem, qualities notably lacking in a great many women.

The women studied by Margaret Hennig spent their early years, she found, developing tremendous amounts of self-esteem related both to their parents' reinforcement of them and their own experiences of mastery and success. It is evidently no accident that so many of my correspondents and of the women I spoke with gave great credit to the supportive roles played by their families; it was also interesting to see how many quoted their fathers during the course of our conversation or correspondence. Since I did not ask them about their family background or their position in the family, I have no way of knowing whether they conformed to the findings of Hennig and others. Because I used criteria of success less limited than theirs, it may be that the pattern would have shown different configurations. There seems little doubt, however, that the only child and the eldest child in a family, male or female, receive more attention and are loaded with higher expectations than other children and, other things being equal, show a higher ratio of achievement, in school and in later life. And it makes sense that a girl competing with female siblings has a better chance of developing competitiveness than a girl competing in a family with male siblings.

It seems, therefore, that some women do have an advantage, within themselves, in striving for success. There are also, it must be emphasized, strong implications in these findings for parents of girls, wherever the daughters come in the family sequence. If self-esteem can be instilled in the first-born, then surely awareness on the part of parents can instil the same kind of self-esteem in younger daughters.

Qualities and qualifications are often hard to separate. Advertisers will ask for a pleasant personality and the ability to type fifty words a minute, for ambition and high school standing, for intelligence and freedom to relocate.

Actually newspaper advertisements are a good guide to qualifications leading to success in business. Since it is abundantly clear that typists' and stenographers' jobs rarely lead much beyond secretarial positions, it is enlightening to read what employers ask for from the women who are to fill the jobs. So I scanned the Help Wanted columns of several newspapers, some in cities with a high level of unemployment and some in cities with very little unemployment, where in fact there was a shortage of office workers and salespeople.

As I had expected, in cities where jobs were scarce employers tended to set forth their requirements coldly and unemotionally:

Typist-Receptionist
Experienced typist-receptionist for local office of firm of chartered accountants. Experience in typing financial statements absolutely necessary. Must be neat and punctual. Salary to be negotiated.

Switchboard Typist Claims Clerk
Minimum Grade 12; 60 w.p.m.; four years switchboard experience. No others need apply. Hours 8.30 to 5.

Experienced Teller
Immediately required a teller with bank or trust company experience. Must be neat and accurate with good customer manner and approach. Should have keen desire for job advancement and be free to accept out of town transfer. Salary based on qualifications and experience.

In cities where there was a shortage of labour, particularly for office work, many of the advertisements were almost cajoling. While they gave the job description and set forth qualifications, they also promised benefits more often than did the advertisements where jobs rather than labour were in short supply:

126

Experienced Key Punch Operator

IBM 029, 129 required for distribution centre in suburban area. Must have 2 yr. exp.

Benefits

- Starting salary generous
- 5 day, 37½ hr. week
- clothing purchase discount
- group insurance plan
- sick leave program
- vac. 3 wk. 3 yr, 4 wk. 12 yr.
- pension plan
- free parking with plug

Executive Secretary

Local mfg. co. located in new industrial park. Large modern office and plant. Air-conditioned. Low cost cafeteria for staff.

Applicants req. to have mastered typing, shorthand, customer relations.

This is a career opportunity & offers the challenge & interest you are looking for. Salary range to $600 a month. All replies confidential.

Accounts Payable Clerk
required by
General Motors Truck Dealership

We offer:
　Attractive salary
　Excellent working conditions
　Employee benefits
　Paid holidays
You offer:
　Pleasant personality
　Neat appearance
　Accounting or bookkeeping experience
Please phone for appointment

Almost certainly all these advertisements were aimed at women applicants. Most typists, receptionists, tellers, key punch operators are female. The salary range for the "executive secretary" and the requirement of typing and shorthand immediately identify the prospective applicants for the "executive secretary's" job. (A true executive secretary should have a secretary of her own to do her typing and to take shorthand notes of meetings and memoranda.) The advertisement for the accounts payable clerk suggests by its list of what the applicant is prepared to offer that it too asks for a woman.

These advertisements all appeared in the Classified section of the newspapers. "Positions," rather than "jobs," were advertised in the Business sections, and more appeared in the Friday and Saturday editions of the newspapers than in the Monday to Thursday editions, presumably because busy people, looking for positions with a future, read the papers with greater care and interest over the weekends. Where the law did not make it mandatory for job advertisements to avoid reference to sex, the large boxed announcements occasionally unashamedly indicated that a man was wanted. A growing awareness of the need to avoid sex stereotyping of jobs was, however, apparent even in provinces that have not yet legislated against discrimination in advertising.

The qualifications for "positions" were generally higher than those cited for mere "jobs." Almost all the advertisements also held out a promise of advancement. In two-column boxes and bold type they read:

Investment Analyst

Financial company requires energetic self motivating individual with effective writing skills for the position of investment analyst at its head office. Academic experience will be either a Commerce degree, M.B.A. or equivalent. The applicant should have a minimum of two years work experience, preferably in investments.

A competitive salary together with a full range of fringe benefits is offered. Applications will be treated confidentially.

Head Office, National Department Store
is looking for
Financial Service Account
Representative

Several career opportunities in financial planning and consulting are available immediately to aggressive sales oriented individuals.

Qualifications:

Grade 12 minimum

Sales experience

Potential to advance to management

Full company benefits and comprehensive training program. Salary range $10,000 to $14,000. Please forward resume to . . .

Energetic, self-motivating, aggressive, experienced, opportunities for advancement . . .

These advertisements were intended to appeal to the ambitious and the career-minded and clearly delineated employers' expectations. My informal survey confirmed what a business executive had told me many years ago. For positions that did not require specific training (accountancy, engineering, law) employers considered successful experience on the job of as much value to them as academic qualifications. Most of them stipulated high school standing only, my informant had said to me, as an indication that a young man or woman had been able to cope with a consecutive and cumulative responsibility, in short, had been able to stick to something long enough to finish it. "And of course it is a guarantee of a minimum intelligence."

Many companies indicated their willingness to train personnel on initial hiring but at the executive level, or in their higher-paid jobs, preferred to take in people who had already received training elsewhere and who were flexible enough to adapt their previous experience to the new circumstances and environment.

In her article in *The Secretary*, Rita Sloan Tilton gave advice to the secretary who aspires to a management position. First, acquire additional training, she wrote, at the local college or university. Express interest in the management training programs offered by the company. Attend professional meetings.

Second, take a personal inventory. Know what you want. Ask yourself whether you are really career-minded rather than job-minded.

Finally, study successful leaders. Decide what qualities and qualifications brought them success, and how they developed these qualities and qualifications.

A Winnipeg woman, twenty-seven years old and working in retail sales, advised: "Apply to an expanding progressive firm. Arrive early, stay late, work hard. Ask questions. Remember the answers; think of a better way. Always be busy. There is always something to do, and the person who cares about the company she's working for will find it. Keep good records of your successes and how they helped to correct your failures. Solve your own problems whenever (almost always) possible, then inform your boss of what transpired. Thus you're keeping her/him informed but showing you are capable of operating independently. Be self-confident and work to deserve that confidence. Know your worth and don't be afraid to ask for it in terms of position or salary. Don't make ultimatums in terms of positions or salary. Be sufficiently well-organized so that you have time in your day for 'want-to-do's' as well as 'must-do's.' Above all, keep your sense of humour."

If I were to distil the collective wisdom of a hundred or more women and a dozen or more men about the qualifications a woman should have for a successful career in business, I would say to her:

- Remember, if you are coming into the labour force after your children are at school, your volunteer work has given you good experience. Build on it.
- Get as much education as possible before you take your first permanent job. Don't overlook the value of part-time work while you are at school and during summer vacations. It provides the experience most employers are pleased to have.
- Find out what you are most interested in doing and prepare yourself specifically for it. Your chances of success are greater if you have specific training, if you know much about one aspect of business.
- Know yourself. Know what you are capable of doing, and set your goals on the basis of that knowledge. Don't underestimate yourself.
- Listen to constructive criticism and benefit from it.
- Look for a role model, but continue to be yourself. It is a mistake to try to imitate someone else.
- Find out what the job you are doing requires and do it as well as you can. It may lead you to something more rewarding if you prove you can handle it well.
- Go beyond the bare minimum requirement both in preparation and in carrying the job load, but don't be a door mat. Be helpful, be diligent, but don't be imposed upon.
- Be realistic about what you can do, but also be optimistic. Knowing you can do something often makes it possible for you to do it.
- If you find you are in a dead end, look for something better, something open-ended.

Having listened, read, and written, I must conclude that the ingredients of success in business for a woman are not much different from those for a man. But to mix those ingredients into the prize-winning cake is far more difficult for the woman. She has greater odds to overcome: her own ambivalent feelings about success; her own definition of success; the traditional concepts of what a woman should do and be; the often well-founded fear on the part of her male colleagues that she is threatening their chances for the prize; her initial positioning in and training for jobs that are static in nature; the feelings inculcated in her from early childhood that the ingredients of success are poisonous for her; her own ability to be contented with what she is doing, or to bear discontent as a necessary burden; her invisibility to her employers as a possible winner.

Theoretically there is no business door closed to women. Theoretically they have the same opportunities for work experience as men. To intimate otherwise is to accept the assumption that there are jobs in business for which men are better suited than women and jobs for which women are better suited than men. "Shame on you!" my friend Gladys Neale answered me when I asked which areas of business offer women the best opportunities. "You should know better than to ask such a question."

Opportunities

Maybe I should have known better, but my observation and my information fed me facts to show that women had moved ahead more rapidly in some areas of business than in others; that large numbers of them had congregated in areas where they made valuable contributions but gained little status and less money; that few of them had encroached on other areas; that few indeed had even ventured into some areas. As a result I decided that there was justification for asking my question.

The young woman presiding over the cash register in a department store thought that key punching was deadly monotonous but recommended "cashing" as an interesting job for other women. The key punch operator thought that the cashier's work was poorly paid and demanding, her own well paid and absorbing. Though many women complained that their pay was low and that men working beside them were better off financially and from the point of view of promotion, relatively few were willing to gamble on a change.

On the other hand, women in work that was once classified as male proclaimed, by their tone if not their words, "Look, I am doing it. Why can't everyone?" and women who would like to break out of the mould of traditional women's work detailed the difficulties they were encountering.

Chatelaine magazine for October, 1974, contained a twelve-page booklet, a "cope-kit" titled "88 Best Jobs for Women Today," prepared by Constance Mungall. Ms. Mungall's list of eighty-eight best jobs was significant for me not for its accuracy or inaccuracy or for the conclusions she drew or the recommendations she made, but because in it appeared so few jobs in business, and because as late as the autumn of 1974, writing in a women's magazine in Canada, she still tended to think in terms of what women are now doing rather than in terms of what they could do. Only here and there did she make a gesture in the

131

direction of the possible rather than the actual, as for example when she noted that Heather Whitehead, in her twenties, was the first woman to trade on the floor of the Toronto Stock Exchange. (She did not mention that there were then about a *dozen* women stockbrokers in Vancouver.) The only business jobs Ms. Mungall mentions are real estate saleswoman, real estate appraiser, and public relations person; someone engaged in business administration, which I suppose covers a broad spectrum of jobs; consumer expert; purchasing agent; stockbroker; sales clerk; direct salesperson; bank teller; secretary; executive assistant; insurance agent; key punch operator; personnel relations officer. Very few of these "best jobs" are not already largely in the woman's domain.

Ms. Mungall was, of course, doing what women are inclined to do: taking the line of least resistance, as counsellors have been known to do, and personnel managers, and teachers of business education. If a young woman wants work it is easier for her to find it in places where many women work, where women are accepted as the norm: in offices, stores, banks and trust companies. Why fight the current? Why spend time and effort and heartache in preparing for jobs that might have to be fought for? So girls, intelligent, capable girls, enter the department stores and supermarkets in droves. Nearly two-thirds of store employees are women; over eighty per cent of management and executive jobs are held by men. "Susan Salesgirl, Dead End Job," Erna Paris called her in a November 1973 article in *Chatelaine*, and went on to say that the job was not entirely dead end. Susan *could* reach a lower-lower management job like head cashier or senior sales clerk.

So girls become typists, stenographers, receptionists, that office trio of invisibility from the mists of which only a rare few emerge to become executive or administrative secretaries, and a still rarer few make it to management jobs, no matter how hard they try – and many do not try.

They enter the banks, like Giuliana, my Italian pupil, with pride that they are working in such responsible positions. Marianne Bossen's study of three major Canadian banks in 1975 revealed that out of a grand total of 3,748 branch managers, 145 were women. Of 234 regional and other senior management people, not one was a woman. Yet women employees outnumbered men almost three to one. Ms. Bossen wrote: "Entry of women into senior management is not seen in the next 5 to 10 years. One bank writes: 'We do feel that our success in moving women into *senior* management positions over the next ten years will depend in no small measure on our success in recruiting management-oriented women from outside.' "[1] By "outside" the bank meant university campuses and their students of business administration. Apparently it was not too optimistic about the women it was training (or not training) on the job, although it, like other banks, was beginning to respond to the pressure of public opinion. Their young women employees are also occasionally prodding them into sensitivity.

"Women's jobs," however, unquestionably provide opportunities, and they unquestionably meet some of the needs of women, or at least the minimal needs of some women.

Let's look at some of these needs, those Ms. Mungall identified and a few others: financial returns, security of tenure, flexibility of hours, home-based work, jobs that demand creativity, status, and prestige.

First, financial returns. Most women, as we have seen, work because they need the money. Most women are underpaid because they do work that is undervalued; and – to come full circle – the work is undervalued because women do it. One of the first items a man discusses with his potential employer is salary; women on the other hand seem to be hesitant about mentioning money, as if it were an indelicate subject to be ashamed of and avoided. Perhaps they have been too long accustomed to doing work without being paid, work at home or volunteer work. Perhaps they are too modest about themselves and what they can do. Perhaps they are insecure because they know how replaceable and inter-changeable they are.

In any event, if they are to take advantage of the opportunities open-ing up for them in business they must overcome their reticence about discussing money. Nor must they place themselves in the position described to me by three or four of my correspondents. These are women who accepted jobs previously held by men at a lower salary than the men had been getting. Even when they asked for a raise and received it, they were still being paid less than their male equivalents. They wanted the jobs; they wanted to show what they could do. And so they permitted the exploitation, sometimes as a matter of course, more often with bitter but silent resentment. Occasionally they fought for equal pay and won their point after they had lost or left the job, but in winning established a precedent for other women in their community.

Governments, federal and provincial, are providing some leadership in abolishing discrimination in salaries between men and women em-ployees, though not enough, Dr. Katie Cooke insists. Unionization of the civil service at all levels has also contributed to a general rise in the salary of women in government offices. Where business has had to compete with government for its female employees, salaries in business offices have frequently shown a parallel rise. An Ottawa businessman complained to me that it was getting "impossible to hire a girl at a reasonable wage. The government pays them so much they think they're entitled to more than they're worth." Where there is no competition for female labour either from government or from industry, the lot of the low-level woman worker is poor indeed, and the young woman looking for a career-type job that pays a reasonable wage is well advised to think of her first job as a clerk-typist-receptionist as strictly part of her training – good training for business, but still training – and to get out of it and, in fact, away from the geographic area where salaries are depressed.

As a sales person she may have better luck. Small population centres often offer better opportunities to independent business people than do the large cities. An acquaintance of mine who saw no future for herself in her routine office job scraped together the money to open a "ladies' wear" store in a busy town within weekend commuting distance of the city and has done very well for herself. Her first job, before she aspired to an office position, was as a saleswoman. In her venture she had the benefit of experience and knowledge of the field. "Otherwise," she said, "I would have been clobbered."

There are, however, opportunities in the stores and in offices and, as has been noted, in banks for those women who are willing to prepare and compete for them. The job of secretary, when it is not merely a fancy title for stenographer, can be a challenge and can pay well. The demand is always high, and promises to grow. Male administrative assistants command excellent salaries; the work done by a female secretary often differs only in title and prestige. Women in these positions are beginning to demand recognition for their worth, and here and there to receive the financial rewards that are the tangible evidence of that recognition. "But DON'T," said a friend of mine who suffered through years of invisibility before her status was raised, "DON'T be bewitched or seduced or what have you by the title. Plenty of girls are being called secretaries and being paid as typists."

Trust companies and other financial institutions are even slower than the banks were to see their women employees as having potential for management; but as one up-and-coming young woman said to me, "We have to embarrass them into doing something. If we are content to take our pay cheques week by week and not ask for anything better, we'll never get it. The boys don't stay in the cages very long. Why should we?" Why indeed?

Ms. Mungall noted that selling real estate and insurance provides good money for women who are suited to the work.[2] It offers a double advantage to those women who must have flexible working hours. Most residential real estate and personal insurance are sold when working people are available to be contacted, and so the job of selling them is ideal for women who can get away in the evenings and over weekends when older children can baby-sit or husbands and other family members are free to take over home responsibilities.

More and more women are, therefore, looking towards realty and insurance as an outlet for their talents and a means of making a reasonable living. Women realtors, however, are quick to point out that unless they are in business for themselves they are almost exclusively in residential real estate and have little opportunity to handle commercial properties, where the high commissions are. Similarly in insurance few women are in the commercial field; their work entails more selling time and lower commissions. Nevertheless both real estate and insurance offer advantages to women because they pay reasonably well, they pay on the basis of the amount of time and effort expended, and the hours are such that women with family responsibilities can cope with home and business both.

Self-employed women encourage others to strike out for themselves, although they take higher risks and only sometimes receive higher returns. There is, however, opportunity for women to establish a firm financial base for themselves if they are interested in developing their own businesses, and many have done so successfully. "It's tough to start from scratch," the owner of a small book shop said to me. "You have to be prepared to starve for a long time until you establish yourself, until you build up a log of regular customers. Very few of us in small businesses get rich in spite of all the help we are supposed to be getting from governments. As I told you before, a woman has a double handicap in raising money initially and in getting loans until her business begins to pay off. Goodness knows, anyone, male or female, has a hard time in the beginning. We women have it that much harder." She added, "But when we make a go of the business there is a satisfaction that goes beyond the financial rewards."

Not all women have the temperament required for self-employment, nor are their circumstances such that they can afford the risk of their small capital. For them security of tenure, the knowledge that the job is there every day and the cheque every week, is more important than the feeling of independence or the distant prospect of higher returns.

135

The need for security was most often expressed, naturally, by those women who had dependants and no means of support except their jobs. Younger women living with their parents, married women whose husbands were working, and women with highly marketable skills that gave them freedom to move around were not as reluctant to give up security for the chance of better pay. They have been brought up in an era where work was easy to get, and money was for spending, not for saving; but to Colleen, deserted by her husband, with young children to support, security of tenure is of paramount importance. Losing a job is a disaster, and the chore of searching for one a searing test of an already weakened self-confidence.

In business there are few jobs with guaranteed tenure, although women's record for staying on the job is good, in spite of the complaint of some employers that their "girls" come and go.

Women who need security in their jobs look for openings where there are pension plans with survivor benefits and protection such as is afforded by maternity leave, sick leave, and group insurance; they are in no position to protest loudly that they are being treated unfairly under the terms of those plans and the protective coverage. Generally they look to the larger companies, since small business firms often cannot afford or have not been accustomed to thinking in terms of such benefits for their few employees. Although unemployment insurance, the Canada Pension Plan and the Old Age Security payments, and prepaid medical and hospital benefits act as cushions, many women are willing to forgo the possibility of higher salaries or greater financial returns in self-employment if they are tied to the risk of short-term jobs.

Unfortunately, young women of promise tend to become lost in the mass of female employees in large companies. Especially if they enter as one of the trio of invisibles, they may live and work to collect their benefits, but the benefits will be small as their pay was low during the long years of their security.

"Get your degree in Business Admin or something – Arts isn't good enough," a bright insurance executive, one of the few, who recently and temporarily, she says, retired into marriage, advised a young friend, "and convince management to hire you as an executive trainee. They're doing it for young men all the time, and they are now being shamed into looking at promising young women. Don't worry about security of tenure at this stage. When you get up high enough you'll lose all security anyway, except what your nerve can supply you with! Show them how good you are. They'll keep you if only to show how liberated they are, and how broadminded. And other companies will approach you if you are really good. The word gets around."

Which is fine advice for those who have the ability to go on and the security or the confidence to give up a sparrow in the hand for two presumptive partridge in the bush, and so I said to the adviser, relating Colleen's predicament to her (p. 35).

"No," she said. "You are not right, and neither was Colleen. From what you say, she is a bright person. She should have swallowed her pride, accepted social assistance or help from Manpower, upgraded herself to the point where she could command a decent salary. Then she wouldn't have been tied for a good part of her lifetime to jobs she disliked. She paid too high a price for the little bit of security she bought with her pride."

Colleen might not agree. She needed her pride and her security, and made sacrifices to preserve them.

These are decisions every woman must, of course, make for herself. But – and this is important – she should be able to make decisions based on sound information. That, I suspect, Colleen did not have at a critical point of her life.

What about the women who feel that they need to be at home, or very close to home, because they have young children or old parents or sick husbands? Some of them have been able to make arrangements for the care of their dependants and have discovered that their need to be at home full time was more imagined than real, that they could cope and their children could cope without their total daily presence. Others have created business opportunities for themselves at home, as Edith did (Edith was the young widow who used her typewriting skills to build a business that now employs up to ten women). Other women with more or less success have supported themselves by selling kitchen utensils, linens, cosmetics, magazine subscriptions, and paintings. A few have built up small home industries, which they now manage: catering; making pickles and jellies; decorating cakes; organizing a handwork co-operative that sells the sweaters, baby clothes, petit point its members make; operating a year-round motel.

Sally ran into problems with her home sales. She knew a good bit about glass, so that over the years her friends had asked her advice about buying or had asked her to buy glass and crystal ware for them. When, like so many others, she found herself in a position where she had to earn money, she decided that her knowledge of glass could be turned into cash, and she was able through contacts she had made earlier to get some glassware on consignment. Gradually her reputation spread, and she built up a considerable clientele. She lived in a residential neighbourhood, and eventually one of her neighbours complained to the authorities that she was carrying on a commercial enterprise in a district that had been zoned for single-family residences only, and probably without a business licence. "That was the best thing that ever happened to me," Sally said. "From being an amateur playing with business – I hadn't really thought of myself as being in business, you see, just obliging my friends as I used to, only getting paid for it – from being an amateur I turned into a businesswoman. I sold my house and got the capital I needed to go into business seriously. This place I am in now is, as you see, a renovated old house. I got it very cheaply and gradually fixed it up. I could sell it now for at least ten times what I paid for it. My apartment is upstairs. I am home with the kids and I am running a very successful boutique, selling more than glass now, of course. You have no idea how much I have learned in the last five or six years."

Marianne Bossen of Winnipeg, born in the Netherlands, with a breadth of experience most of us would envy, is an economist. She too runs her consulting business from her home, a two-storey duplex in an older section of the city. She got tired of working for other people and decided to strike out on her own. Her studies for the Royal Commission on the Status of Women about women in department stores and banks are masterly.

Ailsa has used her homemaking ability to supplement a tiny widow's pension. Over the past several years she has bought and renovated a house every couple of years, living in it during the period of renovation. Every time she has sold the property she has made a substantial profit. "It's like living permanently in a state of having the house painted and decorated," she said, "but it has also been a wonderful outlet for me. The kids pitched in and helped. It's amazing how much of the work we were able to do ourselves; and of course everything we did ourselves raised the margin of profit we made on each turnover. The kids' schooling? You will notice from where I am living that I am in an older neighbourhood. Come, I'll show you the products of our labours. They are all within the radius of a few blocks. We haven't had to give up schools or friends or community."

I have already discussed creativity as one of the qualities that can make for success in business. Creative women like Ailsa have looked to business for opportunities to use their talents to support themselves and their dependants as well as to fulfil their own personal needs as human beings.

Graduates in interior design have found work in department stores, furniture stores, upholstering and furniture manufacturing plants, and are placed with architects. They have set up shops for themselves as interior designers and sellers of furniture and other items of home decoration. Some, like Sally, have specialized and become experts in one field: art objects, china, antiques, imports, books, Canadiana.

Creativity expresses itself in many ways. Advertising agencies employ talented young women. The woman who organized the handwork co-operative is a creative person, and she helps market the work of other creative people. The woman who decorates cakes in her home is also creative; and one of the finest caterers in my city turns out main dishes and confections that are a delight to the eye and the palate, as imaginative, original, and artistic in their way as any more permanent work of art. A cousin of mine who sold hats for many years had a creative touch that could turn a frump into a stately dowager; and many a proprietor of a dress shop has used her talent to attract and hold a faithful following of women. Witness Ms. Miller's devotion to the saleswoman in the department store across the street from her office.

There are creative women in public relations work and writing advertising copy, setting up displays in shops and store windows, designing and writing brochures, arranging interesting tours for travel agencies, designing patterns for clothing manufacturers, and demonstrating make-up in beauty salons. (I watched with fascination one afternoon as a representative of a new cosmetic line made up a mousy insignificant-looking young woman so that she emerged a person of distinction. So skilfully was the transformation done that the young woman looked not made-up but a metamorphosed image of herself.)

Lilian Watson is a travel agent, operating her own business. "Retire?" she said contemptuously. "I won't ever retire. My work is eternally interesting and different from day to day. Handicapped by being a woman? Nonsense!" She is independent; independence is an asset many women would like to have and cannot in the kinds of jobs they hold. She has status, because she is her own boss. The work entails responsibility. Her arrangements have determined the success or failure – almost always success – of the thousands of people whom she has sent to every corner of the globe and thousands, millions of times across Canada.

"If a woman wants to achieve status and hold a responsible job in business she should set her target high, and keep on shooting for it," one of my correspondents wrote. "Let her start out the way the young men do, knowing that she will be president of the company one day." Ms. Mungall in her list of job opportunities for women suggested that in business the jobs that provided status were consultant jobs and administrative positions. It is needless to repeat how difficult it has been for women to reach the upper levels of management from the ranks of most female-oriented jobs. Financial institutions, Kathleen Ruff of the British Columbia Human Rights Committee told me, are the hardest nuts for women to crack. Trust companies, credit and loan companies, insurance companies – among the last to open their doors to minority groups as well – seem to have their own means for keeping women out of decision-making posts.

For the woman who is interested in a high-status position, I can only pass on the advice I have received from women who have, one might say, reached the heights. Avoid, they say, the traditionally female jobs. Look for a niche in business or industry where there are currently few women. Get a solid foothold in that niche, and start climbing! In that way, they say, you will be visible, noticed, commented upon. It will be easier to show what talents you have. You will attract to yourself something of the Queen Bee aura. As one woman among fifty men, you stand out. As one woman among fifty other women, you are hard to spot.

I might say that the advice was not always sound, though it may be now. My cousin Ruth has worked for nearly thirty years in a man's job from which a man would quickly have moved up to the top. The then president of her company told her long years ago when her first boss suffered a tragic death that had she been a man she would have had his job. Twice since then she has been passed over, with expressions of well-deserved appreciation and praise for her ability and thorough knowledge of the job. Eventually she became assistant manager in name as well as fact, with her name listed in the telephone directory and the respect of her colleagues (for what all three honours are worth when the salary does not match the glory). I am told that times are changing.

Women who spoke of themselves as being free of the usual misconceptions regarding women's capabilities sometimes revealed their deep-stamped image of the female role. "Accountancy is a good bet for girls with any mathematical ability," one of my correspondents wrote. "We women are good at detail, better at the meticulous work required of accountants than at making policies." And another wrote, "There are excellent opportunities for women in real estate. It's a natural for women, who are born home makers." And, "I believe that I have been successful in my children's wear shop because as a woman and a mother I understand what children need and mothers want." And, "Women do very well in personnel work because of their special sensitivity." And, on the negative side, "I don't think women make good managers or bosses of any kind. They are petty and demanding. They are better working for other people than having people work for them. So I advise girls to think in terms of becoming a really good secretary, maybe working for an important man and helping him in every way to do his work."

I can agree that being a good secretary is an honourable job, and one which does offer many opportunities for personal satisfaction and for exercising influence on policy, particularly in a small enterprise. Nevertheless, I continue to find myself appalled by the feeling – so often expressed by women or men who have never worked for other women – that women are not suited to managerial tasks.

Anyway, there is no doubt that opportunities exist for women in business that have never been fully explored and exploited. It is encouraging to find that men as well as women are becoming more aware of those opportunities. Both appreciate the loss to the economy when women do not participate to the extent they might and should in Canada's business establishment, especially at its upper levels.

How can women be helped and help themselves to take advantage of opportunities that exist now, or help to create opportunities that are not now available?

It seems clear that as a first step many of them must be re-educated, not in terms of their business skills, but in terms of their perception of themselves. Agencies for that re-education already exist in most parts of the country. Women's groups, with memberships representative sometimes of a broad range of the female community, sometimes of special enclaves with special problems, hold open house, sponsor seminars and discussion groups, operate open-line services for women whose awakening recognition of their own needs have created problems at home and within themselves. Action committees set up to lobby for the implementation of the recommendations of the Royal Commission on the Status of Women have also undertaken educational projects.

Teachers and especially secondary school counsellors have a specific responsibility for informing female students of opportunities in business beyond the traditional trio. Canada Manpower and post-secondary officials must make an even greater effort to open vistas for women, both for the young and for older women returning to work or entering the labour force for the first time. Several provincial governments have women's bureaux, the primary purpose of which is to give information and assistance to women and to employers about women's rights and the opportunities they should have. Employers' associations, chambers of commerce, and men's service clubs must be alerted to the potential their members are underusing. Women themselves must be given every encouragement and support to take the training or retraining they need to fit themselves for a changing commercial world, so that the Colleens do not feel humiliated at the thought of accepting social assistance and older women lose their discomfort at joining young things in the class-rooms of business colleges and community colleges.

The woman who said that a good housekeeper is essential for a woman's success in business was not joking. A great many women could give themselves wholeheartedly to the building of a career in business if they had the same freedom from care as their husbands have; those women who have had the support of a co-operative family credit the family with much of their success at work.

The father who has sole custody of the children of a broken marriage, or who is left widowed with children, is facing the same problems as the sole-support mother. As more men are thrust into a custodial position, there will be more consideration given to the need of the single-parent family, male or female. Meanwhile day care for young children is essential, either at or close to the mother's place of work, or at home, or close to home, so that transporting the children is not a major burden. Mothers of young children should not be torn between the need to be with their children and the need to give undivided attention to their work.

The businesswoman, like any other working person, especially if she is also the head of her household, must organize her home life to con-serve her money, time, and energy. My memory is full of sad tales of young mothers with school-aged children, trying on infinitesimal incomes to run a home, care for the children, cope with an impossible budget, and in some cases hold two jobs in order to make the bare minimum to feed and clothe their families. Because they were not on welfare and had no idea of where to turn for help, they struggled to the point of a nervous breakdown. My contact with them was usually through the school, when the children were brought to my attention because they were falling asleep in class, or were undernourished, or were inadequately dressed for Winnipeg's winter, or were acting out their frustrations and unhappiness on the playground.

These working mothers need both guidance and help. Again women's groups, especially in cities, have organized to provide the guidance and help. Women's centres, operating on a shoestring, have made information available to mothers; women have set up co-operative child care facilities; provincial and civic governments have given some slight support to day care programs and are being lobbied to give more.

None of these efforts, unfortunately, has sufficed to meet the massive need for adequate child care. Legislators have been frank in admitting that most of the provinces could not bear the financial burden of providing for all the children under school age who should be looked after. One of these legislators echoed my own opinion that business and industry, and government as an employer, all of which benefit from the work of women, have a responsibility to help look after their pre-school children. "Look here," he said, "if ABC Insurance Company were employing men in the numbers that it employs women in its offices, and the men had children to care for, the office employees would have organized into a union, or if they are too white-collar to call themselves unionists, into an association; and they would have negotiated day care, for heaven's sake. I'd be willing to bet that it would be economically viable for the company to provide it, too. Think how many girls it trains every year to replace women who leave to have babies. A lot of those women would stay on the job if they could have their children close by, if they had time off during the day to nurse them or give them a bottle or play with them for a few minutes. It costs money to train help. That money could go into day care, and would pay off."

Other countries, such as the USSR, have also made provision for school-aged children to be cared for during lunch hours and after school, so that women can devote their energies and their thoughts to their jobs in the knowledge that their children are adequately supervised. There is no reason why business, industry, unions, and government could not join forces with local authorities to provide the same kind of environment for children in our sophisticated and relatively wealthy society.

As a single woman who has worked for a living all my life I am keenly aware of the disadvantages under which the single working woman labours. A married man with a wife at home to look after him, the house, the shopping, entertainment, his laundry, the home budget has a distinct advantage over a single woman – or man, for that matter – who must cope with all these chores herself – or himself. If she hires someone to do the work, she cannot claim exemption for the outlay of money, though housekeeping help, underpaid as it is, probably costs at least as much as a man expends on the support of a homemaking wife, without the fringe benefits! It is not only the woman with a family who feels that what a woman needs most to succeed in business is a good housekeeper; and I might add, a good secretary.

Fine. Having solved the problems of making themselves available to take advantage of the opportunities opening up for them in business, how do women go about creating some of those opportunities?

In some cases, they have to scout their communities and apply their knowledge of those communities to discover needs that can be filled. That's what Edith did in her university town, and Sally with her glassware business. The women who developed tourist resorts took advantage of a communal need and became successful businesswomen in the process; the woman who used her cooking skills to build up a catering business did the same.

In other cases they have to be bold enough to step out of the crowd and bring their ambition and ability to the attention of their superior officers.

"Why don't women let us know that they want to be considered for other kinds of jobs?"

"We never thought of Miss Z. as a possibility for the assistant manager's job until she told us she wanted it."

"Mary never applied to go on any of our training courses. How could we guess that she was interested?"

Sometimes these remarks are poor excuses by employers and personnel people who had not accepted their own responsibility for seeking out capable women as they do capable men. Sometimes they are cover for not wanting to do anything about providing challenging job opportunities for women. Sometimes they are genuine expressions of puzzlement that women are so reluctant to ask for what they want. Whatever the cause, women should not give employers the occasion for making the remarks.

Furthermore, women should have prepared themselves psychologically as well as educationally so that when opportunities do crop up they are ready to take advantage of them. The woman who has done nothing to upgrade herself, either on the job or on her own time, is not likely to have greatness thrust upon her. Women who have been successful in their work are without exception women who were curious, questioning, learning. When opportunity came along they recognized it and were willing to take a risk in order to grasp it.

To take a risk. Grasping an opportunity always entails a risk; it is never as safe as doing the same tasks over and over again. Virginia

Pangburn, now living in Unity, Saskatchewan, is an example. Her first business enterprise was undertaken at the age of ten.

"I armed myself with a worn-out briefcase of my father's, and sold bedtime story books for children, after school and during the summer. At the age of thirteen I was determined to get into the home of R. S. McLaughlin (the motor people) and sell Mrs. McLaughlin books for her grandchildren. I phoned and told the secretary Virginia wanted to speak to Mrs. McLaughlin. Mrs. Mc. was so intrigued with my ability to get past her two secretaries she invited me to tea. I sold her seventy dollars worth of books, thirty-five of which was mine! Ever since, and all through my life, whenever I have been faced with the need to do something I made a good try at doing it."

Mrs. Pangburn has done many things, most of which her family and others thought she would never be able to do. A few years ago she set up an office in the sun porch of her house and began a placement service for agricultural and household help which eventually developed into her present enterprise: finding work for British immigrants, particularly herdsmen and housekeepers.

"I've done all sorts of jobs in my lifetime from being head cook in a nursing home to collecting for a credit bureau to selling real estate, to what I am doing now, and other things along the way, according to where we were, and what my family commitments were. About the only time I've wished I were a man was when I took my car in for repairs to a place where they didn't know me." (Mrs. Pangburn knows a good deal about cars and trucks, too, and more than once has been able to tell the repair people what to do.) Over the years she and her husband raised a family, living in four different provinces. She has also found time to serve her community as chairman of Housing and Community Planning for the National Council of Women, as secretary and press reporter for the Liberal Association of Fort St. John, British Columbia, when she lived there, as a member of the Business and Professional Club, to name a few of a lifetime of activities.

Her advice to a woman entering business? "If she has the intestinal fortitude a man must have to succeed, she will make it – without women's lib. If she is stupid enough to work for less than she is worth, that's her problem. However, anyone, man or woman, who is not prepared to sacrifice and put forth real effort to succeed, does not deserve to." She added, "My advice to young people starting out is not to be afraid to do something menial if it is the start of their earning career. Not only will it be educationally worth while, it helps to keep them human. By all means get all the training they can acquire; but the one single most important thing in life is attitude. If they are willing to do what is at hand to do, wherever they are, they'll learn a lot, and will become interesting people."

She might also have said, "And will never be bored."

Business, then, has many opportunities for women, some the obvious ones in which many women are currently engaged, some that are waiting to be explored because so few women have considered them possible, some that have to be fought for, some that have to be manufactured through ingenuity, curiosity and research, and some that are simply lying there ready to be picked up by women who have the astuteness to see them and the courage to exploit them. To break out of the traditional moulds is not easy, because the women who try are straining against inner as well as outer constraints; but for the women who have the ability, the energy, the ambition – and let's not forget the luck – the rewards are there: personal satisfaction, financial returns, and – for what it is worth – the knowledge that they are trail blazers.

Miss Brentwood and I met more than thirty years ago, at 7:45 in the morning. We were both waiting for the southbound streetcar to take us to work and struck up a conversation as one crowded car after another left us standing on the windy corner. She discovered that I was a teacher, and I learned that she worked for the Canadian National Railways in an office perched high above and overlooking the vast rotunda of the station. We caught the same streetcar two or three times a week for several years and became quite friendly. Then she retired at the age of sixty during the early fifties on what was at that time a reasonable pension, for a woman, that is, and I moved to another part of the city. Once or twice I ran into her downtown, but years had passed since I had seen her last when one day we found ourselves waiting to be seated in a little restaurant at lunch time. We spent an hour together talking about old times and new, Miss Brentwood surprisingly spry and mentally alert for a woman well on the far side of eighty. She had always been a small woman – I remember she joked about having to be small in order to fit into her little office – and age had shrunk her physically. But her feet were encased in bright red shoes; she wore a smart red pant suit, and her eyes sparkled as she talked.

8

Are the Times Really Changing?

"You've obviously enjoyed your retirement," I remarked.

"Not exactly retirement," she said. "Well, yes, I had to leave my job with the CN. Just in time, too, as it happened. The work I used to do has been completely computerized, and my job has disappeared. Can you imagine me sitting around for twenty years doing nothing? Neither could I. As women's jobs go, or went in my day, mine was good. I was getting paid more than you were in those days, if I recall correctly. I'm a canny sort. I like to spend money, but I know how to save it, so when I retired I had a good nest egg. I went to a lawyer and he helped me to invest it in property – brought in better returns and was more fun to handle than government bonds. It took me a year or two to learn the ropes, and pretty soon I was handling the property myself, buying a little, selling a little when the market was good or I wanted to get rid of a lemon. I have a couple of apartment houses now and one very good commercial building with apartments over the stores. In a modest way I am quite a rich woman; well, maybe not rich, but very comfortable. If I were ten years younger I'd be building the apartment houses instead of buying them."

Here was a very bright woman who had lived through several generations of women in business. Had she noticed any improvement in women's status in the business world? Had there been any remarkable changes in attitudes towards women working, or in women's feelings about themselves at work?

Miss Brentwood had evidently given some thought to the problem of women's rights and women's status.

"Yes," she said, "I can see changes both in the position of women and in their attitudes and in attitudes towards them; or more correctly I should have said that there were changes in attitudes first and then in position. I am sure women are better off in business than they were when I first went to work in 1906. That was a long time ago. We've lived through all that immigration, and two terrible wars, and several depressions. All of them have had an influence on attitudes towards women working. And don't forget the suffragette movement. It's funny how soon all the agonies of it were forgotten and its successes taken for granted. I can remember going to a big suffragette meeting. A bunch of hoodlums came in after the doors were officially closed, and they heckled the speakers. The one man on the platform – I've forgotten his name now – got the worst of the name calling. We were all 'ladies' and I remember being ashamed to ask what some of the words meant. I looked them up afterwards in the big dictionary in the library, blushing all over for fear that someone would notice what I was looking for!

"Anyway, it was during the First World War that we got the first rush of women into men's jobs; so many of the men went off to France. Then bang! when the men came home, the women went home. But not all of them. Just the married ones. Respectable married women simply didn't work in offices. Of course those of us who worked were the first ones laid off in hard times, like during the depression in the twenties. Have you ever noticed the pictures of the Great Winnipeg Strike of 1919? There are almost no women in the pictures, because there were so few women in organized labour at that time. In fact, there were so few women working compared with the numbers employed now. And we knew our place. Did we ever know our place! It didn't even occur to most of us that we should be anything but the bottom of whatever. We were the lowest-paid clerks. We were the lowest-paid servants. What's more surprising as I look back is that we were so grateful for the privilege of being allowed to work and to make an honest living, especially us old maids. After all, we hadn't been good enough to catch ourselves a man."

148

"Has it changed all that much?" I asked her.

She laughed her chuckly little laugh. "Do I hear you saying that it hasn't changed that much? Well, maybe not. But attitudes to women at work *have* changed, and women's attitudes to themselves have changed. You know what really worries me, though? My experience with the suffragette movement. So we fought. So we got the vote. So we didn't use it. So we are better off than we were in 1906 or 1926. But why didn't we pick up from where the suffragette movement left off? Why didn't we take advantage of the freedom we won at such expense and with such wailing about what the younger generation was coming to during the 1920s?

"I'm scared to death that all this business about women's rights and women's liberation will win a battle for us, as the suffragettes did, and in the end we'll be as stupid as we have always been, and lose through indifference everything we have gained."

She asked, "What will happen if we run into another Great Depression? Will the women quietly be let out because – quote – men have families to support? I've never been married, but it burns me up that even now there is an attitude that says loud and clear married women are dispensable or disposable.

"I've always worked mostly with men, and really I'm not sure they have changed all that much. My nephew by marriage was very upset when my niece, who is a capable woman over forty years old, wanted to get paid for the work she did instead of always working for free; she's volunteered for practically everything from Home and School to reading to the blind, and she wanted to know what it felt like to have a pay cheque of her own coming in regularly. He told her she could wait for the old age pension! Over his dead body would she go out to work. She was his wife, and he expected her to be at home. Okay, maybe he's an exception, but if he is there are a lot of exceptions like him. And my great-niece, who is traipsing around Europe with her boy friend – I'm afraid that when or if she marries him she will wait on him hand and foot and give only a second or fifth thought to herself and what she could be. I'm willing to bet that she makes the breakfast now, and washes his socks. If she's like a lot of the young kids I see hiking around all summer she is probably trotting at his heels like a little puppy dog, or like the peasant women in some of our so-called primitive societies.

"Yes, changes have taken place, but slowly, and not completely, and I am not optimistic about their permanence."

"What about the laws that now protect women's rights?" I asked her.

149

"For a long time there have been laws protecting women, that is, singling them out as being different from men, less capable of handling work – like transportation home if they work after midnight. Now there are laws against discrimination in employment."

Again Miss Brentwood laughed. "Laws are wonderful, and necessary, but human nature has a way of getting around laws, or haven't you noticed that? It got around them in my day. Are you too young to remember bathtub gin and bootleggers' joints and bottles under the tablecloth in a restaurant? Human nature hasn't changed very much. The world is still a man's world. The business world is very much a businessman's world. I've lost track of what's happening in the railway, but what'll you bet that there are no more women in the top jobs on the railways than there were in my time? Sure, every now and then you'll see a picture and a big write-up of a woman engineer, or maybe they have a woman on the board of directors – maybe – but the real power is where it always was, with the men. They'll keep it that way. Isn't it in their best interests? Besides, you know as well as I do that deep down in most of their strong masculine hearts they know that they can do a better job than the women. Railroading, even office railroading, is men's work. Hah!" For a small woman Miss Brentwood has an expressive snort.

My conversation with Miss Brentwood took place before I had sent out the questionnaire, which asked whether women in business had noticed any change in attitudes during the preceding five years. It also took place before I spoke with people actively engaged in trying to change attitudes, trying to make sure that women receive the treatment to which they are entitled. In reviewing that conversation months after we had engaged in it I was amazed at how accurately Miss Brentwood, one, two, or three generations removed from the women now deeply involved in the struggle, reflected their perceptions of what was happening.

As might have been expected, women who had achieved a high measure of success in their business careers generally expressed the belief that attitudes had changed substantially.

Marie-Paul Corriveau of Montreal, self-employed in a management role, had written to me: "According to a he-sociologist who studied Quebec women, '75 per cent of Quebec women are liberated but only 25 per cent of the men know it.'" She thinks, however, that changes are taking place, indeed have taken place. "Attitudes to women in business have changed since five years. Even though women who succeed are still exceptional women, they nevertheless have opened doors for other women in the fact that men do not jump in the curtains any more when the Director happens to have a skirt."

Frances Olson, in real estate and insurance in Regina, wrote: "I am treated as an equal by my competitors now – but I wasn't nine years ago."

Kris Kilpatrick, a sales supervisor and buyer in Winnipeg, in her twenties, said, "Yes, most definitely. More and more women are entering the professions leading to business and are not afraid to completely involve themselves."

Rebecca Watson, bank manager from New Brunswick, agrees: "There is a very definite change in attitudes to women in business over the past five years. There is a growing recognition of the potential in capable women. This becomes evident in the business world with more appointments on higher levels being granted to women."

A Winnipeg secretary with forty-four years of experience in the retail field answered: "Yes. I think the young man has been trained or has come to have an entirely different attitude – not the same feeling of responsibility for, but more a feeling of equality with his feminine friends, and this feeling carries on into business and marriage."

Barbara Rae, whose thesis for her M.B.A. degree dealt with women's roles and who describes herself as a general manager and her business as "office services," answered: "Yes. The pendulum has swung far, and women themselves are now faced with commitments that they are not quite ready to make. Culture is slow to change."

Sylvia Lepine of Saskatoon, whom we met in Chapter 3, made a similar comment: "I think there has been an improvement in attitudes by business firms and government offices. What is disappointing is that young women's attitudes have changed very little. Until about age thirty very few women give serious thought to a career, and that is pretty late."

Nan Rajnovich, People News editor of the *Sault Daily Star*, Sault Ste Marie, Ontario, said: "There has been a great change in attitude to women in business, in the sense that the young people who grew up through the peak of Women's Liberation see equality as the natural thing. Some older businessmen have been forced to see things differently. Others will remain set in their ways."

Maxine Avery, bookkeeper in a family hardware business in Yellowknife, believes that "you see, hear, and read about more and more women holding responsible positions in business. Their opinions are valued, and sought after. They are being politically accepted, and perhaps most important, their choice of career is accepted, be it housewife, secretary, accountant, or TV broadcaster."

A young woman, division manager in a large retail chain store, made a valid point: "Yes, there has been an improvement. The fact that a man's wife often works makes it hard for him to ridicule his female co-workers. It is now unfashionable to put down 'the girls in the office' or quote the cliché excuses. Men in many cases still don't want women to get ahead, but the law, public opinion, and fashion make it near impossible to hold us back; and as we succeed, we prove not only our worth but the immense value of women in business. Men are starting to listen to women in business – and that's a BIG CHANGE."

My correspondents differed widely regarding the effects of the women's movement on improving attitudes towards women in business. Gladys Neale was representative of the majority when she expressed the opinion that there has been a marked improvement, "mainly because of publicity, the feminine libbers, the Royal Commission on the Status of Women, legislation, and slowly changing attitudes on the part of both women and men." On the other hand, Anne Stimpson voiced her concern, and in so doing the feelings of a considerable minority, when she qualified her "Yes, there has been an improvement," with the remark that "unfortunately there is too often a militant attitude, an image that will be self-destroying."

I am not sure that my limited investigations bore out Moyra Roberts's opinion. She believes the eastern part of Canada, at least its business segment, has been in advance of the West in recognizing women as people. She wrote from Vancouver: "I think the East, for example Toronto, has been ahead of Westerners in realizing that, in business, women are people too. Companies whose senior staff have Toronto origins seem more amenable to hiring women in 'male' fields." If she is right, times have changed since the days of the redoubtable Nellie McClung, when the West led the country in recognizing women's rights.

Ms. Roberts added, "We still have a long way to go, particularly in the area of being prejudiced against our own sex. We also have to learn to be able to equate the aggressiveness necessary in business with the traditional pull of being a 'lady.' "

Not even dyed-in-the-wool anti-feminists can deny that the past few years have brought a growing awareness on the part of old and young, women and men, that there is ferment in the hearts and minds of women. The Royal Commission on the Status of Women was a major indication both of the ferment and the awareness. The research, the publicity, the involvement called for by the need to make presentations to the commission spread information if it did nothing else; the *Report* and the various debates it generated in seminars, workshops, in newspapers and periodicals, on radio and television, helped spread the word. Many women who had never given the matter of their rights as human beings much thought suddenly found that it was legitimate to voice resentments they had previously buried deep in their unrebellious hearts. They found themselves defending or taking the offensive against positions they had never thought of in terms of defence or attack; in short, they were thinking for the first time in their lives about what they were doing and what was being done to them. International Women's Year, 1975, with all its controversies, internal upheavals, and fiascos, had a similar, if less productive effect. At the very least it proved that the stirring of hopes and feelings is world wide.

I have seen a kind of awareness springing to life in myself and in other women; it is not unlike the focusing of a film which brings into sharp and clear outline what previously had been vague, amorphous shadows, almost indistinguishable from the screen on which they were being cast.

By no means has the awareness been limited to women, or the counteraction, which is in itself a form of awareness, to men. There is hardly an occasion where men and women come together that "women's lib" is not a subject of conversation, in seriousness, in light vein, or in bitterness. Occasionally I hear young girls describing in serious terms plans for their future that do not open with "Then I am going to get married and keep house for my husband and my children. I am going to have a lovely house with English bone china. . . ." Sometimes I hear girls thinking out loud in terms of careers as well as marriage, although, in all honesty, I do not remember any female high school student telling me seriously that she is aiming for a long-time career in business (other than that of being a secretary to an important man).

Four or five years ago I was subjected to a long tirade by a businessman of my acquaintance about the "nonsense of having to advertise for 'a person' instead of 'a girl' " when it was obvious to everyone that what he wanted and needed in his office was a girl. I am sure he no longer gives the matter so much as a passing thought; automatically he advertises for a person, or a typist, or an office worker and not for a girl, a Girl Friday, or a personable young woman. Last time I saw him he told me, a little self-consciously but proudly nonetheless – he was proving that he was "with it" – that he had hired a woman for the first time as a member of his sales staff. He is a wholesaler and used to maintain that his customers would not listen to a woman.

"Oh," I said innocently, "how come? I thought . . ."

"Okay, okay," he interrupted me a little shamefacedly, "so I was wrong. Give me credit for admitting it."

The awareness is growing. There are other symptoms of change.

Women's rights are being seen as part and parcel of human rights. A large portion of the complaints being brought to human rights commissions and committees has dealt with grievances based on alleged or real sex discrimination. Individuals and business companies are sensitive to the publicity that such complaints bring them, and more usually settle them out of court through informal negotiation and discussion. Settlements of this kind set up ripples throughout the business community, so that fewer complaints have to be lodged, in spite of the fact that more women employees are becoming conscious of their rights under human rights legislation, or equal pay and equal standards legislation.

Another symptom of change is to be found in the right that women have won – or more accurately discovered, since no law exists to the contrary – to continue to use their maiden names after marriage. That concession has automatically removed, in provinces where it has been made, the requirement on some application forms that the maiden name of the applicant be given, a sexist remnant that permitted personnel officers to identify female candidates for positions.

Many married women have also insisted, and in insisting have made the point, that as working women they are entitled to credit without benefit of their husband's signature. The battle, I am told, is not completely won in all provinces. My informants and friends tell me that even when they have had ten years or more of tenure in their employment, and in some cases earn more money than their husbands, retail stores, automobile repair shops, finance companies, and banks initially refused them credit on their own signatures. "But things are looking up," I was told. "I still sometimes have to make a fuss about it, but I don't face the stone-wall resistance I used to get when I applied for a credit card as a person in my own right and not as my husband's wife."

"Or my father's daughter," another woman added. "I had been working for three and a half years in one place and was living on my own, when I went to buy my own car. I blew up when the sales manager wouldn't arrange credit for me. He wanted my father to guarantee my signature. No way, I told him. I'm an orphan, I told him, lying in my teeth. Either you sell the car to me, as I am, or you don't sell it. He called my boss; he checked my bank. By that time I had bought my car somewhere else. Stupid. After all, the finance company would have had a lien on the car. My brother, who is far less reliable than I am, bought an expensive car from the same outfit without a bit of trouble. I boycott any outfit, and I let my friends know about it, that refuses credit just because I am female."

"Many companies are now only too pleased to have women's business," one of my correspondents wrote, "and I find that there is much less discrimination in the granting of credit than there used to be."

"Business firms have come to realize how important women are to them both as consumers of products and as employees. Even the sexist advertising aimed at us is in its way a compliment to the control we exercise over the money that is spent in this country," another wrote. "As a part-time worker and part-time housewife – I am proud of the title – I have noticed considerable change in the approach to me in both my capacities. I belong to a small committee in our town that monitors advertising and television shows as well as commercials. Women are still being treated as morons in many of the TV commercials, but more and more the shows are beginning to pay lip service to us as people to be reckoned with in business and the professions. Since the media are responsive to the lowest level of public thinking, I am encouraged to find women appearing even as tokens in roles of leadership. I am a little concerned that this is happening much more consciously and frequently in American productions than in Canadian ones. Or maybe I am just more sensitive to what is being produced in Canada."

"It may be that 1975 being International Women's Year there is more writing about women in different roles than there used to be," said another of the women I talked with. "Whatever the reason there has been a spate of letters to the press, and every magazine and 'People's Section' of the newspaper carries something regarding women's position in the professions, business, etc. I started keeping a file of clippings and soon found myself overwhelmed. Not all the material is pro-female, of course. There has been a big and often snide counter-wave coming from men and women who feel threatened by female militancy. I heard a chap on the radio the other morning holding forth on how the women were getting very pushy, and didn't they know that their pale imitation of masculinity made them neither male nor female but like the competent eunuchs the Turks used to keep in their harems. When I called the radio station to let them know what I thought of that particular speaker I was put through to some young squirt who told me that I was proving the speaker's point! I was fighting mad, but just the same the fact remains that the question is being debated and widely debated instead of being laughed at or, worse still, ignored."

I showed the Royal Bank booklet to a male acquaintance with many years of experience in the banking business. He has always deplored the waste that he saw of women's potential. He looked through the booklet and said, "Well, you must know that this is a pretty accurate portrayal of what actually happens in a bank. I don't suppose it has changed fundamentally in the two years since that pamphlet was planned and published; but I am encouraged. Even if the few women in managers' positions are tokens, even if very few hold top jobs in banking, there is still a feeling of discomfort growing in the banking establishment, or at least in the lower ranks of the establishment. I guess even we men begin to feel uncomfortable when our noses are rubbed in the injustices we have been perpetrating. I am hoping that change is coming, in fact is well on its way. Not that I expect we will have a woman president in our bank within the next short while, but the possibility can be talked about, which is more than could have happened even five or six years ago."

Marianne Bossen concludes as a result of her study of employment in chartered banks, 1969 to 1975, that there has been a noticeable change in Canadian banks: "Our analysis of occupational data leads us to conclude that the position of women in the banking system has improved since 1969, both quantitatively in branch line management for example, and qualitatively, in the sense of a stronger participation at junior and middle management equivalent levels in operational and staff functions. We believe that the improvement has been brought about by the expansion of the banking industry in the past six years, more enlightened executive policies (in some banks more enlightened than others), and a positive response from women to opportunities offered." From 1969 to 1975 the number of bank branches increased by 19 per cent, the number of women branch managers by over 500 per cent.[1]

"I was delighted," a young mother said to me, "to see out on the shelves in my daughter's Grade 2 classroom a whole series of little pamphlets showing both men and women doing a variety of jobs. It was such a pleasant change from the textbooks we have been examining as part of a community project in our school district. The teacher, a very bright young lady, told me that more and more material is becoming

156

available that shows women in non-traditional roles . . . and men too. However, she also told me that the children in their drawings still showed the strong influence of the world 'as it is' and not as she and I would like it to be. A funny thing she mentioned – in several pictures kids drew of their visit to the school medical room to get their shots the doctor appeared as a man, although the school doctor is a woman, and aside from the principal who dropped by occasionally during the inoculation process, there actually wasn't even a man in the room! I suppose their pediatricians are all male, and so when they drew a doctor they automatically drew a man although the doctor who was doing the inoculations was a woman. Or more likely they just think of a doctor as being a man and the nurse as being a woman."

Some of the leaven has reached the colleges and universities. Although they have been unconscionably slow in remedying the injustices to be found in their own staffing policies they are beginning to make a notable contribution in other ways, not the least of which is the establishment of courses in management specifically for women. These courses, directed to women already holding management positions or preparing for them, are anywhere from a few days to a year or more in length. York University, for example, held a seminar for women in management during the autumn of International Women's Year, and the ongoing offerings at Algonquin College in Ottawa are typical of many such programs across the country. They propose to make women aware of possibilities for them in management and to help them acquire the techniques and procedures that will help them reach executive status.

Since it is good public relations nowadays to show no discrimination against women, even conservative businessmen are beginning, sometimes reluctantly and with reservations, to appoint women in places where they will be noticed. Like one of Canada's department stores in the bad old days, which made sure that it had at least one Jewish employee so that it could not be accused of anti-Semitism, Canadian business establishments are apt to have a woman somewhere to whom they can point in order to prove that they are not anti-feminist, and – cross their little hearts – have no bias against moving women into positions of responsibility. It remains for these showpiece women to prove their worth and to help others break down the barriers they were helped over.

"Tokenism can be a dreadful business," a former "token" appointee said to me. "I own a few shares in a local company. I knew very well when I was offered a seat on the board of directors that it was a gesture, a public relations deal, and that I wasn't expected to do anything except sit and look interested. But I made up my mind that I was going to make a contribution to that company whether they wanted it or not! So I made myself thoroughly knowledgeable about the business. My appointment was made six years ago. I am sure that no one now thinks of me as a 'token' member of the board. Last year I was elected – unanimously, if a little grudgingly by one or two members – I was elected vice-chairman. I participate actively in the concerns of the business."

"My advice to women is to take any job that is offered to them, token or not, and then make something of it," the male president of a small manufacturing outfit said to me. "How are you going to show us that you can do a job unless you take it on? Tokenism isn't limited to females, you know. We have several deadheads, male, at the top of our company, mostly family members that we have had to provide for. A word of warning to token female appointees, if you don't mind. Tell them not to start pushing too soon. Easy does it. Tell them to make themselves a part of the picture before they do too much talking."

Quite aside from token jobs there are many more opportunities opening up for women in the last quarter of the century than there have ever been, as my correspondents kept reminding me. Secondary and postsecondary educational institutes are permitting, if not always urging, girls and young women to train themselves for jobs for which formerly only the exceptional female would have been considered, and the aspirations of many girls have been changed considerably as a result of the gradually changing climate.

The enactment of anti-discriminatory legislation has been both a reflection and an implementation of changing opinion regarding woman's place in the working world. Although this legislation is not comprehensive, and varies from province to province in its coverage, strength, and enforcement, it has been a powerful tool in helping women to appreciate their own value and in impressing on employers the need to recognize that worth in tangible ways. Combined with pressure from the women themselves it is helping to force a re-examination of what until recently had been accepted as routine: discrimination against girls in the schools through the content of textbooks, library books, athletic programs; inequalities and inequities in company benefits such as group insurance, pensions, and participation in health and other insurance plans; hiring on the basis of sex; exclusion of women from clubs, associations, and other groupings through which business contacts are so often made; and – a most important element of discrimination against

158

women – lower pay for women than for men in jobs with comparable work loads and responsibility.

But in my exuberance at the changes that have taken place in attitudes towards women in business, let me not overlook or forget completely Miss Brentwood's words of warning. Her doubts and reservations were shared by many of the women who wrote and spoke to me.

"Let's not kid ourselves," said a young woman who has worked in several "female" jobs – switchboard operator, office girl, typist. "These changes of attitude are very much on the surface. Many places are afraid of the publicity if their true practices are exposed, and so they make a gesture in the direction of equal rights for women. No woman in any of the places I've worked has ever gotten out of the rut she started in, no matter how intelligent she was or how hard she tried. In one of the offices there was a woman who had her name on a door; she was secretary to one of the big shots. I know from a friend who worked on the payroll that she didn't make nearly as much money as the lowest-ranking young man in the office. He was called an executive trainee."

V. E. Morrison of Thornhill, Ontario, personally cannot see any great changes in attitudes to women in business during the past five years. "I feel women hold such few positions [of authority] because men are not prepared to share the top influential positions with women, as they wish to remain superior."

Jean Tweed of Toronto, asked whether she thought there was a change in attitudes to women in business in the past five years, answered succinctly: "No. A lot of talk; not much action."

From Vancouver came a comment: "If there has been a change it has not been noticeable to me."

Jean MacDonald, in real estate in Montreal, like several others believes that attitudes are changing and that more opportunities are opening up for women. "Not enough as yet, though, as there are many capable women listed as 'executive assistants' who are doing the work of vice-presidents but not getting the salary or the recognition. This *must* be changed."

A Frenchwoman, also from Montreal, wrote, "It is not much use changing attitudes if we women don't take advantage when we are asked to do something different from what our men have always expected." This thought was expressed many times. Donneda Morton, Winnipeg, wrote, "Yes, attitudes are changing, but many women are still too insecure and lacking in confidence due to lack of training and always feeling the pull of family responsibilities."

I became used to the remark from women that they could hardly expect male attitudes towards them to change when they themselves were changing so slowly. For example, a woman of thirty-five or so said to me that she had only just become aware, when she went back to work after nearly ten years at home, that there were any inequities in the treatment of women. "It was only after listening to a couple of the young kids in the office holding forth that I realized there was anything wrong. One of them took me to a seminar about women, and I felt like a fool. What they were talking about was so obvious, but no one in our circle of friends had ever thought in those terms. My husband certainly never thought that the girls in his office were being badly treated, and I was actually grateful that I was given the opportunity to be exploited! We've had some red-hot arguments at home in the last couple of years. I've given him literature to read. He was either angry or pretended to make fun of it at first, but he is a very intelligent man, my husband. He's on my side now. He's even coming to the meetings with me, though usually he is the only man there. I was thrilled when he made his top girl an assistant manager instead of bringing in a young chap from outside for the job."

How deeply and firmly set are women's attitudes has been demonstrated to me repeatedly. The counsellors in the school in which I worked had told me how solidly traditional most of the girls were in spite of a surface commitment to women's rights. I proved the counsellors right over and over again, as I talked with fourteen- and fifteen-year-old girl students.

As Sylvia Lepine had found with her business education students, few of my junior high school girls thought of work as anything but a stopgap before marriage; few of them saw themselves as partners in a marriage in which their presumptive husbands would share in carrying home responsibilities.

"You are both going to be working during your first years of marriage," I said to several girls. "You both leave the house at eight in the morning and come home after five in the evening. What happens then?"

And the answer was the same, whether I put the question to a youngster from a well-to-do home where both parents were professional people or to the daughter of a blue-collar worker. "I'll get dinner, we'll eat, I'll wash up, and then we'll have the evening together."

"And what will your husband be doing while you are making dinner, washing up, and so on?"

"Well, he'll be watching television [or reading the paper], having a beer [or a drink, or a cocktail] before dinner."

"Won't he help you get dinner or with the dishes after dinner? After all, you were both working all day. Why should you come home and go to work again?" I asked.

The answer to this question varied a little, but not much. Occasionally one of the girls replied cheerfully that, yes, her husband might help dry the dishes. Her dad sometimes did; and he would carry out the garbage. Or she might say, "Dry the dishes? Oh, no, that's not a man's job. He'll cut the lawn or shovel the snow until the kids are big enough to do it. And, oh yeah, he'll carry out the garbage, sometimes."

"In those early days of your marriage you might be living in an apartment, and there would be no lawn to cut or snow to shovel, and the building super will do the other odd jobs like fixing the taps. Shouldn't your husband be helping you with the housework?" And more often than I would have believed the reply came quickly, "Oh, no. That's *my* job. I *want* to do it."

How long did they propose to work after marriage?

"Oh, a couple of years, till we get enough to buy a nice car [or make a down payment on a house or buy nice furniture]. Then I'll settle down." I am sure I heard those words a dozen times – "I'll settle down and have a family, maybe one or two kids."

"Will you go back to work when the children are at school?"

Well, they weren't sure. Probably. Of those who said yes, they would, the majority had mothers and fathers who both worked outside the home.

The occasional girl said she was interested in a lifetime career, almost without exception a professional career. Not one girl up to the age of fifteen of all I spoke with seemed to think of a career in business as being a long-term commitment; those who had selected business education as the next educational step saw themselves as rising to the height of being a secretary. One girl, whose mother is in business, when pressed said doubtfully that it might be "nice" to own and operate a boutique.

What did they think of the women's movement? "Women's lib, you mean?" one long-haired, lithe young lady asked. "I believe in equality with men. I think we should be paid the same as men for doing the same work." She spoke firmly and with conviction. But she was also one of the girls who didn't think it was a man's job to help with the dishes.

The father of one of the girls I had talked with told me later that he was having trouble with his daughter. "I hope you aren't filling her full of that women's lib nonsense," he said to me sadly. "She fights with her brother all the time and has taken to telling me off in no uncertain terms when I ask her to help her mother around the house. If it's not you people in the school giving her these crazy ideas it must be the stuff I've caught her reading lately. Awful stuff. I don't think it should be allowed."

I am, of course, describing extremes. Or maybe I am not. The fact remains that even very young women find it hard to accept new roles, to see themselves as whole persons, with value in the social, political, and economic structure that is entirely divorced from their relationships to their husbands, fathers, or brothers.

Indeed, if Marnie Clarke of the Ontario Women's Bureau is right, there is more movement and more change among middle-aged women than among the very young. Young women, to quote Catherine Bowell of Canada Manpower in Toronto, too often have the feeling that they will always be looked after, that they will get married and be protected forever after. This, in spite of what the experience in their own homes should often have taught them.

So change is coming slowly. More talk than action. Sylva Gelber points out that in relation to their numbers very few women are reaching the policy-making levels of business. The fact that here and there women of note reach the high places is of little real significance. Always, in all countries, the position of women in the upper classes bears little and frequently no relationship to the general status of women. So it is that the example of countries where women have reached the presidency or the prime ministry proves nothing in terms of what is likely to happen here.

Which means that the tokenism which earlier was described in positive terms can also be a negative manifestation. "See! We don't discriminate against women. Why, we have appointed Mme Y. to the Board," or "Miss B. is a bank manager in that nice little branch on the university campus. We've done our duty by you."

Miss Brentwood voiced her concern about faddishness. Right now the women's movement is fashionable, as several of my correspondents also noted. What happens when interest dies down, as it has in the Students' Rights movement? What happens if women do not take advantage of the battles they have won, do not claim the equal opportunities and the equal rights other women have fought for? Will they go by default?

Nor has the countermovement been stopped. As the books and magazines pour out information about women, the disabilities under

162

which they function in today's business world, their need for equal consideration as people, other books and magazines – sometimes the same magazines and newspapers – are pouring out the counter-propaganda, on an equal-time basis.

The countermovement finds support in the feeling of guilt many women harbour within themselves when they leave their homes and, in the minds of friends, neighbours, family, shuffle off their responsibilities to their children in order to earn money. It is also supported by the need for self-justification on the part of those women who truly want to make home and family a career. (They should not, of course, have to justify their choice of career any more than the businesswoman should have to justify hers. It is a legitimate, worthy, and important option.)

Change of traditional attitudes towards women is also slowed down by other societal factors and by the cyclic nature of our economy. Women do bear children; and those children do have to be cared for. As has already been pointed out, our society makes very little provision for care of children even when it is imperative for economic reasons that their mothers work. When my aunt, sixty years ago, was widowed, my grandmother took over the nurture of four young children. When a friend of mine lost his wife fifty years ago his maiden sister came out from England to look after his orphaned children. Employers and governments are refusing to face the facts of life: grandmother is rarely available these days to take on the burden of a young family. She is working herself; or she lives hundreds of miles away; or if she is elderly she is safely tucked away in a senior citizens' residence. Maiden sister is not prepared to sacrifice her own life and career to look after her brother's or her sister's children. Paid day care is both expensive and inconvenient when it is available, and it is in short supply. Therefore expensively trained, capable, economically valuable women stay home to provide the day care that cannot be provided in any other satisfactory way. In so doing they deprive the economy of their skill, put their employers to the expense of training new workers to replace them, and often frustrate themselves. In spite of token efforts here and there, like the Manitoba government's limited subsidy of day care, little has been done to remedy this particular situation or to remove this particular handicap from women in business who have children to care for.

The economy itself plays tricks on women. The cataclysms of history have also contributed to keep working women on a breath-taking roller coaster. When men have better things to do, that is, when they go off to war, woman's work is in great demand. During both world wars Canadian women filled the gap left by men joining the service, and on a wave of sentiment returned home to have their babies. Except for those who had acquired a habit-forming taste of life outside the confines of their homes, or who had made so valuable a niche for themselves that they could not be spared, or who had lost potential husbands in the mass slaughters and had to remain at work, or as always, those who had to work in order to eat.

Meanwhile the business world particularly had become heavily dependent on the cheap work of women. That work formed the base on which the traditionally male stronghold of business now rested. In spite of this dependency, or perhaps because of it, a male stronghold it remained; nor did it occur to the masses of women to storm the stronghold. Such married women as remained in the white-collar labour force after the wars ended were victims of recurring economic depressions. When jobs are scarce, women are the first victims except in those jobs which employers, less than philanthropic, consider totally female in character and do not offer to men even in periods of high unemployment.

Women are themselves part of the society that patterns them, and there may be almost as many women as men who are content with the status quo, who indeed may believe that the world is moving too quickly towards change. Women of all ages and at every social and economic level resist change, and some are actively ready to combat it when it threatens their comfortable position. As economists, male, point out to us, to pay women on the same basis as men would put a severe strain on the economy; almost certainly to pay women for the work they do as housekeepers would change radically the social and economic balances.

I would find the economists and the sociologists who are disturbed by women's demands for equality of treatment more convincing if I had not read similar prophecies of doom from advocates of child labour at the beginning of the nineteenth century, and the opponents of universal education and universal suffrage at the end of the nineteenth century. At this period in our history we should be more concerned with moving towards the improvement of women's condition than with the problematic havoc the improvement might create. If that concern is to be transformed into action it will be through the acceleration of those forces that are now operating and through an exploration of other means of influencing women and men, of changing deeply engraved cultural patterns.

The drive for this acceleration and exploration must come from women, informed, active, intelligent, concerned women, working in conjunction with equally informed, active, intelligent, concerned men, but themselves providing the leadership. Radiating from the present nuclei of Status of Women committees, business and professional women's clubs and associations, Women's Institutes, trade unions with predominantly female membership, local, provincial, and national Councils of Women, there should be developed a series of "cells," small, intense, highly motivated groups of women and men who have as a primary objective the spreading of information first among women and then among the whole community.

One complaint about women's movements has been that they are made up mainly of middle-class women, many of them discontented housewives, welfare mothers who have a particular axe to grind, and the far-out characters who represent small minorities but make a lot of noise. Maybe these three groups have been most vocal. Maybe the working women in low-paid jobs have not been as easy to reach; they *are* working women, most of them with two jobs – one revenue-producing and the other home-making. Maybe these other women who appear infrequently at women's meetings are less articulate. If the accusation is true that they are not being represented in women's movements, then a first duty of the "cells" is to reach them, to find out why they are underrepresented, to bring them information which they may not have. I know, from having talked with women at all levels of employment, that very few like to be exploited. Their problem is that of the majority of women: they are shy; they are modest; they do not want to be thought brash or pushy. That is why I advocate a small unit to which they can be invited or brought by someone whom they trust.

The influence of the family on a woman's chances of success in business has been mentioned several times. If there are going to be effective changes in the rearing of girl children – and of boy children for that matter, because nothing will change for girls unless changes take place in boys too – the process must begin before the children are born. Pre-natal counselling of parents is of primary importance; it is particularly important to involve prospective fathers in the pre-natal educational plan. Their part in the raising of their daughters is, as Margaret Hennig, Marjorie Lozoff, and others[2] have made abundantly clear, of crucial importance to the children's future.

Children cannot choose their parents, but parents can be helped to instil in their daughters the qualities that will enable them to take a richer, more rewarding part in building the kind of country they want to live in and to claim for themselves a fair share of the rewards of their labours. When more mothers stop preparing their daughters for the marriage market and turn their attention to developing them as persons, when more fathers stop treating their daughters as mothers' little helpers and think of them as individuals with brains and ambition, girls will be less reluctant to take on job responsibilities, and their brothers and potential husbands will be more likely to think of them as equals in industry, business, and the professions.

Departments of education, school boards, textbook publishers, and teachers are becoming increasingly sensitive to the effect of sex stereotyping in schools, but much remains to be done in providing suitable materials, in re-educating teachers from nursery school through college to the fact that girls do not have to be passive and accepting, boys active and dominant, that women as well as men have made a contribution to history and are making a contribution, too often unrecognized, to economics, politics, business, industry. I have at hand a book about Manitoba pioneers, for example, compiled by a panel of women, and 267 pages long. Only three women were considered worthy of entry, one the mother of the first white child to be born in the West, one known for her good works as the wife of a prominent man, one because she had the foresight to keep a journal which – as is so rare in our history – sets forth the day-by-day work done by an ordinary woman in laying the foundation of a new nation. That journal might teach us a lesson. I discovered in collecting material for this book how difficult it is, in spite of a growing literature, to find anything about Canadian women in specific occupations. Perhaps we should be encouraging women today to keep journals, and to have them published. History, as I have already noted, has almost universally been written by men about men. We should also be encouraging women biographers and researchers. *Ms* magazine has run a series of articles about "lost women," women whose achievements are unknown or were unknown until *Ms* brought them to light. Canadian women, in business, at home, in the professions, need the same kind of attention.

Schools are a convenient target area. They are accessible, vulnerable, and influential. They also have a responsibility for presenting many points of view, partly to reflect our cosmopolitan national composition, partly to encourage critical thinking in our students. I am not suggesting that the educational system be subverted to propagandize women's rights and women's story; I am saying that it should be rid of the bias that is now prevalent in it: a bias which helps to maintain serious imbalances in our understanding of the human condition.

It may be that schools have another responsibility, to business directly. Both business and labour have a legitimate complaint that the secondary schools, particularly, have for generations tended to place too much stress on education for the professions· and not enough on the other options open to most girls and boys, business among them. There has also been a tendency to channel mainly non-academically oriented students into business education programs, a procedure which further tended to downgrade business as a legitimate and desirable career for women who were looking for a challenging occupational choice. Business educators tell me that there are signs of change here too, but as elsewhere it is needlessly slow in coming.

Newspapers, journals, radio, television, films have played an ambivalent role in helping women achieve success on equal terms with men. Most newspapers in Canada have replaced their Women's sections with People's or Family sections, or have used similar changes of title to meet the complaints of women's groups. There has not, however, been much change that I have noticed in the content of the People sections, or the Family sections. If we need a special section for the Family, or the People, at whom is the rest of the newspaper aimed? The stories of successful businesswomen tend to appear not in the News or Business or Financial sections of the newspapers but in the re-named People or Family sections. The very fact that the appointment of a female manager of a supermarket or a bank branch appears as a news item is in itself a form of insult.

Television over the past several years has provided us with a few women in glamorous jobs of some status: lawyer, doctor, police chief, journalist, spy (or whatever the current name for spy happens to be), mother-performer-cook; but in the business field women are still secretaries, occasionally the powers behind the male thrones, but normally the bearers of information, the makers of reservations, and the fearful protectors of their menfolk. Nowhere is tokenism so rampant as in television, small tokenism, at that.

Women have had and can have a marked influence on what appears on the television screen, in the form of both entertainment and advertising. Because television, with some exceptions in the Canadian Broadcasting Corporation, is commercially oriented, it must respond to what its viewers think of it. If Nariman K. Dhalla is any guide to how merchandisers regard the female market, we shall continue to see ourselves as vapid creatures. "A typical woman," he writes, "is not so keenly interested in winning the admiring glances from men as in having

167

reassurances of her femininity and good taste. Probably the most effective method is to create an atmosphere of romance, an aura of happiness in companionship, the feeling of loving and being loved. Also, motherhood means more to a woman than wifehood. Both physically and mentally, she is intimately and inextricably bound to her creation. As a result, advertising campaigns revolving around pictures and stories of mothers and children seldom fail to gain immediate attention."[3]

Businesswomen, then, should be convincing advertisers that they are not moved to spend their money when they gaze at advertising that reassures them of their femininity and their good taste, or appeals only to their capacities for motherhood. Mr. Dhalla, who is billed as a marketing and research director, does go on to say that the large number of women at work outside the home has implications for marketing, and that working women have needs that differ from those of the women who are at home (also working). These women now represent a large share of the buying public. Surely television and other advertisers should be aiming at them the kinds of programs and commercials that would reflect new self-concepts and different life styles from those we are accustomed to seeing on the home screen.

Groups of citizens, male and female, have had removed from television commercials propaganda they considered discriminatory, pornographic, or merely tasteless. The most effective method has been to write, in large numbers, to the heads of companies sponsoring the advertising; to appear where possible as delegations to these heads of companies; to present not hysterical tirades based on emotional reactions, but carefully reasoned arguments against what they found objectionable backed up by suggestions of the kinds of advertising which might sell the product.

If this approach is taken, behind the objections should always stand the possible sanctions against buying the product because of the objectionable advertising. Since much of the advertising is national in scope, a campaign of this nature requires co-ordination of effort, no small task: the co-operation of men and women not only in business, but in trade unions, social and fraternal organizations, and the support of the various media because this kind of campaign must have publicity.

An attack on advertising that denigrates women has threefold value. In addition to removing the debasing material from the air, the attack itself becomes a means of spreading information, of rousing awareness in women as part of the total population, of educating the viewing public. It also places upon the advertiser and the public relations agency a responsibility for replacing the discarded commercials with more suitable, more intelligent advertising which then in turn becomes a form of education and communication of ideas about women.

Legislation has a part to play in accelerating change of attitudes towards women in business, indeed towards women at work of any kind. While it is true that laws do not work unless they have the support of the people over whom they are exercised, as my friend Miss Brentwood was not the first or only person to point out, they would never have passed the legislating body if they had not had a considerable body of support. Once enacted, they, like the anti-advertising campaign, have an educational effect. Their promulgation informs employers and employees alike of what the body politic considers acceptable hiring practices, for example. The penalties they often include deter would-be offenders and encourage would-be complainants. Often legislation sets up investigative bodies whose functions are also to inform, to deter, and to enforce.

Very few of the businesswomen with whom I spoke or corresponded advocated legislation that would enforce "affirmative discrimination," that is, that would make mandatory the hiring of women in certain proportions in certain kinds of positions, or the compulsory enrolment of certain proportions of women in management programs. Some women like Zelda Roodman and Sylva Gelber, however, were firmly convinced of the need and found good reasons for legislative action in favour of women. In no other way, they said to me, would women overcome the strong sanctions built into our society and our economy against their movement upward – and outward for that matter – into areas still largely shut off for them. The process of change, if left to hit-and-miss efforts on the part of women and interested men, is too slow, and ultimately too costly, for the women who are being deprived while it is taking place and for our society and economy, which suffer the loss of women's intelligence and ability.

Terry Pickles of New Westminster, British Columbia, put the case like this: "Society will have to discover that we women have a right to become part of the productive structure of our country and give us what we need to become part of this structure. I am afraid that the situation demands affirmative legislation on the part of government unless we are prepared to wait many more years than necessary for this integration process to occur."

Personally I have ambivalent feelings about reverse discrimination. Not least of the reasons for these feelings is my distinct and unpleasant memory of the horrors of quota systems that were used until recently, and may still be used covertly, to limit the numbers of unpopular or minority groups entering professions like law or medicine or chartered accountancy. I find the very word "quota" distasteful when it is used in the sense of limiting access to employment or schooling. Affirmative or reverse discrimination immediately calls for quotas, in a good cause, of course, but quotas nevertheless, and quotas based not on ability to handle jobs but on a factor that we insist should not be taken into account in hiring or promotion policies, that is, sex. To repair one injustice by institutionalizing another does not make sense to me. Just as it is now grossly unfair that girls and women of ability are not being considered for certain jobs in the initial hiring or promotion, it is unfair for capable men to be passed over in order to fill a female quota.

On the other hand, I cannot help but be moved by the argument that it is equally and grossly unfair for women of ability to be deprived of opportunities right now because they are not being hired for or promoted to positions currently filled by men of lesser ability. My militant friends are impatient with what they call my shilly-shallying. I tell them that I have been encouraged by what has happened in the schools during the past half-dozen years: girls are more interested than they once were in running for student offices and are being elected with some regularity. In the awarding of prizes and scholarships it is no longer common practice, as it was until recently, to award prizes to the girl and the boy with the highest standing in the school; the prizes are now awarded to the two students with the highest standing, without consideration of their sex. Surely girls and boys brought up to think in terms of equality of opportunity will reflect these attitudes in later life.

"Not good enough," they insist. "We don't want to wait. Besides, you yourself have shown us how conservative the younger generation is. We have to do something *now*, and it has to be drastic if change is to take place at all. As for putting capable men out of jobs, that's nonsense. Use your head. In a very short time the level of ability in most positions should rise, because instead of making selections from half the population, selections will be made from the total available pool of men *and* women. The chances of getting high-quality people for high-quality jobs will be almost doubled. Anyway, what makes you think that the men displaced to make room for women would be more capable than the women replacing them? Do we detect traces of some of the stereotypes you complain about in others?"

So there I am.

In spite of some of my misgivings regarding the legislation of reverse or affirmative discrimination in favour of women, I am convinced that the law should and can be used to remove discrimination, as it is already being used slowly and often reluctantly, but still used. Examples of this kind of use appear in the news daily: the University of Regina must give retroactive pay to its female cleaners in order to equalize it with the pay of male custodians, the judge ruling that equal work is not necessarily the same as identical work; the Nova Scotia Human Rights Commission undertakes a study of women's access to credit; provincial governments produce booklets to inform women of their legal rights, and set up women's bureaux to serve women at work; federally and provincially paid women travel about the country drawing attention to needs and proposing remedies. All these are the results of legislative action. Governments have also helped the cause without the need for specific legislation: retraining of teachers, sensitivity to curricular content and teaching approaches, a slowly growing recognition within the federal and provincial civil service commissions of women's right to participate at higher levels than the clerical. (Municipal governments seem somehow slower to react.) Law reform bodies are making recommendations and governments are considering reforms in the realm of family law and property rights of married women.

The barriers against women are still high and the barricades strong. Legislation, federal, provincial, municipal, is required to extend and enforce equal pay, to provide better and more extensive day care for children of business and other working women, to remove inequities in the Canada Pension Plan and insurance provisions in private plans, to make certain that upgrading opportunities are as accessible to women as to men, to prevent discrimination against working mothers, to inform and to educate employers.

To repeat what I have already said, women themselves must help one another to break down the barriers and to scale the barricades. Through their own organizations and on a personal one-to-one basis they must accept responsibility for informing, educating, pushing and pulling eligible women. Like the token female, the Queen Bee serves a purpose. She is visible; she is capable; she is, in spite of herself, a model for girls who admire her accomplishments. But the Queen Bee is also an enemy in that she is likely to keep herself aloof from the struggles of other women; she has no patience with those who need help on the way. It has been encouraging to meet so many successful businesswomen who are not Queen Bees, who do accept responsibility for their female colleagues, who offer help and – even more important – encouragement, who recommend women for positions they are able to fill, and urge women to apply for these positions.

The greatest obstacle to change still remains the business community and the attitudes of many businessmen. Even here change is becoming apparent, as my correspondents testified; but if the change is to be accelerated the momentum must come from business people, particularly businessmen who hold the reins of power, tightly and with no noticeable desire to relinquish them or jeopardize the grip on them. As my militant friends pointed out to me, it is going to be a long wait if women have to depend on the changes in attitude that are now being inculcated in schools and colleges. The young girls into whom we are trying to instil self-confidence and career ambitions, the women whom we will be urging to prepare themselves for a future in business will be frustrated and angry if they run into a stone wall of resistance of the kind I encountered in my interviews with so many businessmen: "It's all right for you to argue about women's place in business, but I must tell you that I prefer my wife – and my daughters – to be at home where they belong. Oh, of course, there are women who can do men's work, but frankly I don't like them." They are the characters who almost convince me that affirmative discrimination is necessary and must be imposed by law.

It is incumbent on their colleagues to re-educate these people in order to prevent government intervention. It will surely take place if they remain obstinate in the face of growing militancy on the part of working women and, I hope, of growing sensitivity on the part of the rest of the population. The process of re-conditioning, or de-conditioning, the business community is not easy. The very nature of the task makes it one in which male co-operation is essential.

Debbie Lyon, writing in the *Winnipeg Free Press* in the summer of 1975, quotes Bluma Appel, special assistant to the federal minister of health. Ms. Appel is a successful businesswoman, sitting on the boards of three companies. She talks to women's groups, but her main purpose is to reach men in top executive positions and convince them of the value of having women in similar positions. Ms. Appel is quoted as saying about these executives she approaches: "They lose touch. I want to arouse their consciousness . . . to let them know that there's something new, something exciting happening. . . . They're not evil. They really want to do the right thing. And they're finding out how to do it. It's a

172

totally new thing for them." (I can't help but wonder why it is so new for them.)

Initially, she said, there's curiosity; sometimes she has to overcome fears or prejudices; sometimes there are polite battles; "but by the time I go they usually see the implications of what's happening."

Ms. Appel, like me, is convinced that discussion is better than open war. She disapproves of, though she understands the reasons for, boycotts of companies discriminating against women. "Discussion takes longer but it does not leave the same residue of bitterness and resentment."

Men who are sympathetic with women's struggles for recognition in business have the same duty that Ms. Appel has to talk with and by example help to convince their more traditional colleagues, individually and through the numerous male-oriented organizations into which businessmen are banded. Women cannot afford to wait until the "under thirties" reach positions of power. Ms. Appel thinks the "under thirties" have been affected by the atmosphere in which they were (presumably) raised so that they "don't know that women are supposed to be inferior to them."[4]

I share Miss Brentwood's concern that once the flurry of interest is over, businessmen will settle back into their comfortable old ways with a sigh of relief that they are no longer being bombarded by those impossible females. It is essential that the bombardment become heavier rather than cease and that it come from men as well as impossible females. Male speakers on the subject of women in administration and management every month or two at a service club luncheon can imperceptibly but effectively influence their "brothers," although I am not above using charming personable women to vary the audio harassment.

My suspicion is strong that the economic argument brought forward by some of the men with whom I talked carried less weight, even with them, than the emotional set they had against women in positions competitive with their own. If I have no respect for the argument it is because I have heard it used so many times in so many contexts to oppress the already oppressed, and because no business that I know of has suffered materially as a result of paying women at the same rate as men. Instead the policy has attracted better people, male and female, lowered the turnover rate in predominantly "female" employment, and generally raised the standard of living for many workers.

Women white-collar workers have been urged to join trade unions in order to better their salaries and working conditions. Trade unions, however, are as conservative as business employers in their attitudes to change in the status of women. Perhaps therein lies another good reason for increased female membership. Marchak found that "unions as they are presently constituted are no help to most white collar women." She drew the conclusion that the failure of unions to organize white-collar workers to a greater degree was probably due to discriminatory attitudes on the part of union organizers and male union members rather than to disinclination on the part of women to join unions.[5] If she is right (or more correctly was right, since her study was carried out in 1969), the task of de-conditioning unions is at least as great as that of convincing businessmen; and the responsibility for carrying it through, as with the latter, must be shared by female unionists, by male union members, and by the unions as a body. Women should be able to count on the union movement to win and defend rights for them that are not even questioned as being the rights of all men.

For attitudes to change substantially in a short period of time, then, requires a large commitment on the part of most of society: government; the schools, universities, and colleges; the family; the business community; the unions; women's organizations; interested individuals male and female.

Ultimately, however, every woman is going to have to make her own choice as an individual; she will have to decide how she feels about herself, what she wants to do, and how much she is willing to do and to give up doing in order to achieve what she wants. If I were speaking to a woman at the critical point of her decision making, I might say these things to her:

After all, it is pleasant and comfortable to fill a well-defined and respected role, whether it be that of wife and mother, or clerk, or secretary in a situation where someone else makes major decisions. Especially if you have been brought up to expect courtesies from men, to have small tasks done for you without the need to ask, to have others bother their heads about meeting expenses, running a business, dealing with employees, there is not much attraction in the thought of undertaking these duties and responsibilities if you "don't have to" – that is, when there are no financial pressures on you to take them on.

Then there is the sense of guilt to overcome if you have the courage, or even the financial need, to break away from the traditional roles. Guilt at neglecting children, if you have any; guilt at separating yourself

174

from, or even competing with, your husband, if you have one; guilt at intruding yourself into situations where you are often obviously unwanted, where the laugh is stifled, or the topic of conversation changed, because you are suddenly an unwelcome woman in a man's domain; guilt at being "unwomanly," "unfeminine," and therefore unattractive (you think or are made to feel); guilt at breaking away from traditional cultural and family expectations, thereby separating yourself from friends and family.

And there is the genuine concern about the value of making a choice that leads to stresses and strains, perhaps not greater but certainly different from those you would experience at home or in a job without much responsibility. Do you want, you ask yourself, to fall heir to ulcers or heart attacks or hypertension, the ills that male go-getters are supposed to suffer from? "Look," one of my friends said to me, "what would I gain if I went out after a department manager's job? Nothing but heartache, and maybe a heart attack. Let someone else who likes that kind of tension get the job. It's not for me. The extra money doesn't compensate for the dirt I'd have to take."

You may believe that there is a genuine conflict between your success in business and the care you want to give your children. There is no question of guilt, because you have already made the choice that home and family are of greater concern to you; and because your job will always be secondary to you there is no need for you to move onwards and upwards. In fact, you deliberately decline any move that will take you away from your undemanding low-level work.

So in the end the choice is a personal one: to decide what you want to do with your life, and to determine for yourself at what niche you are content to stop; to make up your mind to what extent you wish to identify yourself with others, men and women, who have the same ambitions and philosophy as you have; to choose the degree of commitment you have to your career, whether at home or in business.

If the choice leads you to look for a job in business, you know the obstacles you have to overcome, and the sources from which you can draw assistance. One of the greatest obstacles is the excuse, well-supported by easily obtained evidence, that many women are not interested in advancement, do not have the same interest in a successful, progressive career as their male colleagues. This excuse you will have to dissipate by your own actions, regardless of the encouragement and support you may receive from family, colleagues, women's organizations.

Decide what field of business interests you most. Make your decision wisely, in the sense that you allow yourself considerable range for experimentation. Work during your high school years and your time at college, after hours and during the summer vacations. If you are not happy with one kind of work, stay with it long enough to know why you do not like it and then try something else another summer. Several kinds of experience are useful to you no matter what you decide to do later in life.

Then – or even before you go to work – prepare yourself for the kind of work you want to do. Although a strongly feminist friend of mine insisted that I warn girls against taking typing and getting into a dead-end job, make sure that you learn to type. As with work experience, the ability to type is useful whatever work you later decide to do. Remember, too, that education is no longer considered a finite activity. Educational doors remain open to you as long as you live and want to walk through them. If you find yourself in a job that seems to lead nowhere, think of improving your skills at night school; consider upgrading yourself, or changing your work direction by attending a community college. If you see yourself heading for management, your employer may be willing to finance part of your attendance at one of the many business administration and management courses available for short and long periods of time.

It helps to have tangible proof of your upgrading. Membership in an organization such as the National Association of Secretaries, for example, which issues a certificate testifying to your proficiency, is a fine recommendation if you want to move from the stenographic pool to the boss's office. A degree in business administration or commerce is an indicator to a prospective employer, or to prospective clients if you are in business for yourself, that you have invested time, money, energy, and thought to prepare yourself for a long-term career.

Do whatever you have to do on the job as well as you possibly can, and cheerfully. If you see changes that can be made, make your suggestions through the proper channels, and constructively, being careful of the sensibilities of those whose policies you are challenging.

There are ways of making yourself visible, of making known to those people who hold the power of promotion that you are in line, willing and able to take on additional responsibility. No one should have the excuse that he did not know you wanted a job, or cared about it. As so many successful women have advised, get out of a job that leads nowhere if you want to go somewhere. Change employers, if your current employer thinks of you as one of an indistinguishable mass.

176

Apply for positions that look interesting to you and that you think you can handle. Do not be discouraged when you do not get the positions. The experience you gain in being interviewed will stand you in good stead. Think of every application that is not accepted as an instrument for learning. You will gain confidence as you go along if you don't permit yourself to feel crushed by your failure to get the jobs. Thank your interviewer for the opportunity of being considered, and ask him to keep your name in mind. If you are really interested in the job, call back occasionally to find out whether there is another opening. Keep an eye and an ear open for job opportunities that may come to your attention before they are advertised. You have a better chance with someone who knows you and the quality of your work, ambition, and energy.

As for losing your femininity because you want to succeed in your work, don't worry about it. Your femininity is a part of you. Being subservient is not being feminine; being self-confident and assured is not being unfeminine. I could never understand why it is acceptable for a woman to be confident and self-assured about her appearance, her dress, and her manners and unacceptable for her to be confident and self-assured about her intelligence, her ability to do a job well, her business acumen.

Don't give up easily. You are going to need more staying power than your brother, your boy friend, or your husband. You will have to be less sensitive to rebuffs, and often more patient.

And keep your sense of humour. You are going to need it.

Epilogue

From four o'clock to six the elevators in the tall shafts of office buildings slide up and down, up and down, carrying their bright cargoes. Little shops and huge corporations pour into the street the throbbing current of the business world. Drained of it, they stand empty and moribund, chains of light in high windows telling of cleaning women and night watchmen preparing for a renewed influx tomorrow morning. In shopping centres and corner grocery stores, in supermarkets and co-operatives, cash registers still click open and shut, as money passes from hand to hand; busy tellers check deposits and pay out cash in banks that accommodate night shopping clients, until they too wearily complete their balance sheets and make their way home through the late evening twilight. From the mists of the West Coast to the mists of the East, from the long winter nights of Inuvik and Yellowknife to the fruit country of the Niagara peninsula, on the prairies, in mountain valleys, in smog-draped cities and tiny villages, women have covered their typewriters, counted their receipts, cleared their desks, watered the plants, and regretfully discarded the last rose in its glass vase. Their business day has ended. How many of them know that without them the business day could not have begun? How many of them realize the power they have, these Cinderellas of our economy, these stepchildren of business? May their daughters and their granddaughters remember them with honour and not with pity, with respect and with wonder at their patience. May the world in which their daughters and their granddaughters live and work feel astonishment at their exploitation. May they remember so that hard-won rights are not lost through neglect. May they count success in terms of satisfaction in work well done. May they retain the self-confidence and self-esteem that make any job interesting and rewarding.

May many more of them than their mothers and grandmothers sit in the executive suites of business, in leather chairs and behind mahogany desks. May many more of them rate name plates on their doors, and recognition on their companies' letterheads.

These Cinderellas will not need a prince and his glass slipper, a fairy godmother and her magic coach. They will have the intelligence, the education, the motivation, and the drive to make it on their own.

178

Notes

Chapter 1

1 Labour Canada, *Women in the Labour Force*, 1975 ed., p. 37.
2 Ibid., pp. 24–25.
3 Ibid., p. 49.
4 Labour Canada, *Women in the Labour Force*, 1973 ed., p. 49.
5 Labour Canada, *Women in the Labour Force*, 1975 ed., p. 49.
6 Ontario Ministry of Labour, "Fact Sheet, Working Women in Ontario – 1973."
7 Statistics Canada for Labour Canada, Women's Bureau, quoted in Canadian Press release, 19 March 1975.
8 Ontario Ministry of Labour, "Fact Sheet."
9 Sylva M. Gelber, "Notes for Panel Discussion at the Annual Meeting of the Canadian Sociology and Anthropology Association, University of Toronto, August 25, 1974," *INFORMATION*, p. 10.
10 Labour Canada, *Women in the Labour Force*, 1975 ed., p. 287.
11 M. P. Marchak, "The Canadian Labour Farce," in Marylee Stephenson, ed., *Women in Canada*, p. 209.
12 RCSW Studies No. 9, Renée Geoffroy and Paule Sainte-Marie, *Attitudes of Union Workers to Women in Industry*, p. 115.

Chapter 2

1 RCSW Studies No. 8, M. D.-Johnson, "History of the Status of Women in the Province of Quebec," in *Cultural Tradition and Political History of Women in Canada*, p. 6.
2 A. Oddson, *Employment of Women in Manitoba*, Appendix A, Table 3.
3 *Winnipeg Free Press*, 18 Jan. 1975.
4 Oddson, *Employment of Women*.
5 *Canada Yearbook, 1959*, p. 742.
6 In *The Secretary*, April 1974.
7 Labour Canada, *Women in the Labour Force*, 1973 ed., p. 239.
8 *FACTS*, 1973.
9 Labour Canada, *Women in the Labour Force*, 1975 ed., p. 21. There is a discrepancy in the figures here due to different ways of collecting data.
10 Ibid., p. 37.

RCSW, Royal Commission on the Status of Women in Canada

11 John Porter, *The Vertical Mosaic*, pp. 80–81.
12 Labour Canada, *Women in the Labour Force*, 1975 ed., p. 31.
13 Ibid.
14 Ibid., p. 37.

Chapter 3
1 Labour Canada, *Women in the Labour Force*, 1975 ed., pp. 155, 168.

Chapter 4
1 M. P. Marchak, "The Canadian Labour Farce," in Marylee Stephenson, ed., *Women in Canada*, p. 207.
2 Labour Canada, *Women in the Labour Force*, 1973 ed., p. 115.
3 Canadian Press news report, 23 Jan. 1968.
4 *Winnipeg Free Press*, 3 Aug. 1974.
5 Ibid.
6 *International Women's Year* 2, no. 5 (June–July), 1975.

Chapter 5
1 Brenda Sivers, *let's pretend we work in the bank*, p. 14.
2 Manitoba (Govt.), News Service, "Job Satisfaction Is Major Women's Goal, Says Survey," 9 Aug. 1974.
3 M. M. Kimball, "Women and Success: A Basic Conflict," in Marylee Stephenson, ed., *Women in Canada*.

Chapter 6
1 M. P. Marchak, "The Canadian Labour Farce," in Marylee Stephenson, ed., *Women in Canada*, pp. 203–12.
2 See Margaret M. Hennig, "Family Dynamics and the Successful Woman Executive," in Ruth Kundsin, ed., *Women and Success*.

Chapter 7
1 Marianne Bossen, *Employment in Chartered Banks*, p. 39.
2 Constance Mungall, "88 Best Jobs for Women Today," *Chatelaine*, Oct. 1974.

Chapter 8
1 Marianne Bossen, *Employment in Chartered Banks*, pp. 19–20.
2 See Ruth B. Kundsin, ed., *Women and Success*.
3 Nariman K. Dhalla, *These Canadians*, p. 112.
4 *Winnipeg Free Press*, July 1975.
5 M. P. Marchak, "The Canadian Labour Farce," in Marylee Stephenson, ed., *Women in Canada*, p. 209.

Bibliography

Alberta, *Individual's Rights Protection Act* [enacted Jan. 1, 1973].

BERGMANN, BARBARA R. "The Economics of Women's Liberation," *Challenge, the Magazine of Economic Affairs* 16, no. 2 (1973).

BLISS, MICHAEL *A Living Profit: Studies in the Social History of Canadian Business, 1883–1911.* Toronto: McClelland and Stewart, 1974.

BOSSEN, MARIANNE *Employment in Chartered Banks, 1969–1975,* sponsored by Advisory Council on the Status of Women and the Canadian Bankers' Association. Ottawa: 1976.

BOWELL, CATHERINE "Women and Work" [a series of papers]. Toronto: Ministry of Labour (Ontario), 1974.

British Columbia. *Human Rights Code of British Columbia Act* [enacted by British Columbia Legislative Assembly Nov. 1973].

——— *Report of Human Rights Branch* (Kathleen Ruff, Director), 1973.

——— University of British Columbia, Centre for Continuing Education. *Report – Western Conference/Opportunities for Women.* Vancouver: University of British Columbia and Vancouver Status of Women Council, 1973.

Canada, Department of Labour, Women's Bureau. *Women at Work in Canada: A Fact Book on the Female Labour Force.* Ottawa: Queen's Printer, Information Canada, 1964, 1973, 1974, 1975.

——— *Women's Bureau* [issues for 1970, 1971, 1972, and 1973].

——— *Women in the Labour Force: Facts and Figures* [issues for 1971, 1973, 1975].

——— Department of Labour, Economics and Research Branch. *Working Conditions in Canadian Industry, 1972.* Ottawa: Information Canada, 1972.

——— Royal Commission on the Status of Women in Canada, Studies. [Bossen, Marianne.] *Patterns of Manpower Utilization in Canadian Department Stores,* No. 3. Ottawa: Information Canada, 1971.

[Bossen, Marianne.] *Manpower Utilization in Canadian Chartered Banks,* No. 4. Ottawa: Information Canada, 1971.

Cultural Tradition and Political History of Women in Canada, No. 8. Ottawa: Information Canada, 1971.

[Geoffroy, Renée, and Sainte-Marie, Paule.] *Attitudes of Union Workers to Women in Industry,* No. 9. Ottawa: Information Canada, 1971.

DHALLA, NARIMAN K. *These Canadians: A Sourcebook of Marketing and Socio-economic Facts.* Toronto: McGraw-Hill, 1966.

181

EASTHAM, KATHERINE *Working Women in Ontario.* Toronto: Ministry of Labour (Ontario), 1971.

FARMER, GERALDINE M. "Business Education in Canada: Critical Problems and Exciting Prospects," a paper presented at the Second Canadian Conference on Business Education in the Secondary School, Niagara Falls, Ontario, April, 1969 [unpublished].

——— "My View of the Emerging Profile of Canadian Business Education," in *An Emerging Profile, CABET 1973* [a collection of papers delivered at the Fourth Canadian Conference of CABET]. Toronto: Gage, 1974.

GELBER, SYLVA "Equality in Pensions for Working Women," *Women's Bureau '73.*

——— "Notes for Panel Discussion at the Annual Meeting of the Canadian Sociology and Anthropology Association, University of Toronto, Toronto, Ontario, August 25, 1974," *INFORMATION* [Department of Labour, Canada], 1974.

——— "Organized Labour and the Working Woman," *Women's Bureau '73.*

——— "Quebec's Contribution to the Status of Women in Canada," *Women's Bureau '73.*

——— "The Rights of Man and the Status of Women," *Women's Bureau '73.*

——— "Time to Reform Traditional Insurance Practices to Eliminate Sex Discrimination," an address to a meeting of management, Manufacturers Life Insurance Company, Toronto, Ontario, 1974 [unpublished].

GREENGLASS, ESTHER "The Psychology of Women or the High Cost of Achievement," in Marylee Stephenson, ed., *Women in Canada.* Toronto: New Press, 1973.

HALL, OSWALD and MCFARLANE, BRUCE *Transition from School to Work.* Research Program on the Training of Skilled Manpower. Report No. 10. Ottawa: Department of Labour (Canada), 1962; reprinted, 1965.

International Women's Year 2, no. 5 (June/July, 1975). Ottawa: International Women's Year Secretariat.

JANEWAY, ELIZABETH *Man's World, Woman's Place: A Study in Social Mythology.* New York: Delta Books, 1971.

JOHNSTON, JEAN *Wilderness Women, Canada's Forgotten History.* Toronto: Peter Martin, 1973.

KIMBALL, MEREDITH M. "Women and Success: A Basic Conflict," in Marylee Stephenson, ed., *Women in Canada.* Toronto: New Press, 1973.

KUNDSIN, RUTH, ed. *Women and Success, The Anatomy of Achievement.* New York: Wm. Morrow, 1974 [originally published under title *Successful Women in the Sciences*].

LORING, ROSALIND and WELLS, THEODORA *Breakthrough: Women into Management.* New York: Van Nostrand Reinhold, 1972.

LOZOFF, MARJORIE M. "Fathers and Autonomy in Women," in Ruth Kundsin, ed., *Women and Success, The Anatomy of Achievement.* New York: Wm. Morrow, 1974.

Manitoba, Department of Labour, Women's Bureau. "Facts and Figures on Working Women in Manitoba," Winnipeg, 3 March 1973.

—————— *Mothers in the Labour Force, Their Child Care Arrangements.* Winnipeg, Sept. 1974.

—————— [Government] News Service. "Job Satisfaction Is Major Women's Goal, Says Survey," 9 August 1974.

—————— *The Human Rights Act* [received assent August 13, 1970].

MARCHAK, M. PATRICIA "The Canadian Labour Farce: Jobs for Women," in Marylee Stephenson, ed., *Women in Canada.* Toronto: New Press, 1973.

MELTZ, NOAH M. *Changes in the Occupational Composition of the Canadian Labour Force, 1931–1961,* Department of Labour (Canada), Economics and Research Branch, Occasional Paper No. 2. Ottawa: Queen's Printer, 1962.

MUNGALL, CONSTANCE "88 Best Jobs for Women Today, A Chatelaine Cope-Kit." *Chatelaine* (Oct. 1974).

ODDSON, ASTA *Employment of Women in Manitoba,* Project No. 18, Economic Survey. Winnipeg: Manitoba Economic Survey Board, 1939.

Ontario, Ministry of Labour. "Summary of the Interim Report of the Task Force on Section 4(1) (g) of the Ontario Human Rights Code," October, 1974.

—————— Women's Bureau. "Fact Sheet, Women in Management," October 1972.

—————— Women's Programs Division. "Fact Sheet, Working Women in Ontario – 1973."

—————— Provincial Secretary for Social Development. *Equal Opportunity for Women in Ontario, A Plan for Action.* Toronto: 1973.

—————— *The Ontario Human Rights Code* [received assent February 1974].

PATERSON, EDITH "Margaret Scott Devotes Life to Winnipeg's Needy," *Winnipeg Free Press,* New Leisure Section: 18 Jan. 1975.

PORTIGAL, ALAN H., ed. *Measuring the Quality of Working Life: A Symposium on Social Indicators of Working Life, Ottawa, March 19 and 20, 1973.* New Research Initiatives Research and Development Program. Ottawa: Department of Labour, 1973.

Provincial Council of Women of Manitoba. "Report of Chairman of Trades and Professions," Winnipeg, May, 1974 [unpublished].

SIVERS, BRENDA *let's pretend we work in the bank.* Toronto: Psycan Ltd., 1973.

STAINES, GRAHAM, TAVRIS, CAROL, and JAYARATNE, TOBY EPSTEIN, "The Queen Bee Syndrome," *Psychology Today* 7 (Jan. 1974).

Statistics Canada, *Canada Year Book, 1959, 1965, 1970–71, 1974*. Ottawa: Queen's Printer and Information Canada, 1959, 1965, 1971, 1974.

—— *Labour Force by Marital Status and Age Group*, Advance Bulletin, 1971 Census of Canada. Ottawa: Information Canada, 1972.

—— *Occupations*, 1971 Census of Canada. Catalogue 94-717, Vol. III, Part 2. Ottawa: Information Canada, 1974.

TILTON, RITA SLOAN "The Future Secretary's Perspective," *The Secretary* (April 1974).

Winnipeg Chamber of Commerce, "Submission by the Winnipeg Chamber of Commerce to the Business Education Task Force, Department of Education, Province of Manitoba," December 1974 [unpublished brief].

WALKER, KATHRYN E. and GAUGER, WILLIAM H. *The Dollar Value of Household Work*. Social Sciences–Consumer Economics and Public Policy No. 5, Information Bulletin 60, New York State College of Human Ecology, Cornell University. Ithaca, N.Y.: n.d.